LINUX

COMMAND

*Logical and Systematic
Approach to Linux
Administration*

WILLIAM VANCE

Table of Contents

Introduction

Linux refers to a group of operating system distributions that are built around the Linux kernel. Linux refers, in a stricter sense, to the presence of kernel itself. If you want to build a complete operating system, Linux distributions include viable tools and libraries in its GNU project and allied sources. More and more developers have started using Linux recently to build and run a wide range of mobile applications. Linux also has played a key role in building some affordable devices like Chromebooks. These devices run the operating systems on the kernel. Linux has become a popular choice among developers and common users due to some practical reasons. The top reason is that Linux distributions always remain current and are supported by the communities of a wide range of developers. Linux runs on a diverse range of hardware systems, and it will install alongside the pre-existing systems. This is a helpful trait in local development environments, supporting the installation of centralized software and with low resource requirements. It often comes to mind whenever developers start building some kind of application ecosystem, server tools, and higher levels of compatibility. It usually sustains all the necessary modifications for operating system behavior.

Open-source software is no longer considered a privilege that only developers and tech-brains can have access to. You do not have to become a programmer to enjoy open-source software. Linux is gradually gaining popularity among the masses largely because it is free. Linux can be traced back to the free and open-source software movement. As a consequence, developers chose it for ethical and practical reasons.

It all started with Unix, which is one of the most popular operating systems across the world because it has a large support base and big distribution. Originally, it was developed as a system that could multitask for small computer systems in the 1970s. Since then, it has grown into one of the most widely known operating systems across the world even though it has a confusing interface and an absence of central standardization. The reason behind its popularity is that lots of hackers feel that Unix is the best operating system. An expanding group of Unix hackers developed Linux, which is a branch of Unix.

Linux became a free-of-cost distributable version of Unix, developed by Linus Torvalds. He now maintains the Linux kernel that is considered as the lowest-level core component of an operating system. The first version of Linux was released free on the internet. Gradually, it gained the position of the biggest software development phenomena in the world. Nowadays, it is being maintained by thousands of developers that have been loosely collaborating across the internet. Lots of companies have sprung up out of nowhere to give Linux support.

What This Book Has to Offer

This book touches upon the topic of Linux administration from different angles. I have tried to include all the relevant topics so that you will be no stranger to the Linux operating system.

Note: The book is divided into two major parts. The first half of the book focuses on Linux commands. You will have to open up the Linux terminal to try and see the result of each command when you go through this section. Afterward, the other half of the book focuses on scriptwriting in the shell. For this purpose, you will have to install a text editor, of which I have done a comprehensive discussion and review in the relevant chapter. You also can run an online text editor for Linus to practice different scripts that I have written in the book. If you try to run a script in the shell, it will not work.

Similarly, if you try to run a command in the editor, it will not show the desired result. Keep a Linux terminal and text editor on in the computer system to make the most out of it. You can copy the commands and the scripts and paste them in the shell and editor respectively to see how they work. Upon successful execution, you can make some edits in the script and try to create your version of it. This is the most viable learning strategy. Practice is the key to learning Linux.

The book is divided into different long and short chapters, each containing content of its type. I will give you a brief introduction of each chapter so that you can have a knowhow of what the book contains and how it can help you in your journey of learning Linux.

The first chapter of the book will introduce you to different aspects of Linux, such as the abstraction layers, the system hardware, the kernel, and userspace. I will give you a brief introduction of each so that you know what you need before you enter the world of Linux. On top of all the must-haves is a not so high-end computer. As Linux is more about programming and coding and less about the graphical interface, you need an average machine to perform efficient programming functions and to run different types of software on the system without slowing it down.

The second chapter of the book introduces you to Linux commands. The real fun starts here. I will explain the first keys that you can use. I will also explain what the shell window is. Understanding the power of the shell window is important as it is the shell window that you will see most of the time for your day-to-day operations. I will explain it in detail before moving on to the basic shell commands. In the next section, I will shed light on the file system. Unlike a Windows operating system, Linux has a centralized file tree system which you have to navigate with the help of the Linux shell system. For example, if a file sits in your system and you do not know about its type, you can write the type command in the shell screen and know the type of the file. With simple commands, you will be able to view the content of the files on the screen of your operating system. In the next section, I will shed light on some random commands which you will need the most during your daily operations. The first on the line will be the ls command that explores a file or a directory. The cp command works for copying the contents of a file into another file. The touch command is the next, while the mv command is the last. The mv command moves the contents of a file into another file. Linux allows you to navigate through different directories in the blink of an eye. I will go on to explaining more commands such as the mkdir command, which is used to create a new directory. I will also explain the rm command that can remove a directory from the system. The chapter ends on the explanation of the ln command.

The third chapter of the book is where I will practically explain how you can navigate around commands. I will give you a detailed definition of commands so that you can bring them into practice in the Linux shell. This chapter contains details on more complex commands than that of the previous chapter. The first command on the line is the man command, which allows you to go through the document of different commands and files. The man command denotes the manual of different commands in Linux. After explaining it, I will move on to the apropos command. The next on the line is the whatis command. In the end, I will explain how you can create a command with an alias. This is the most interesting thing in Linux. When you have created an alias in Linux, you can use the same instead of writing the complete command. Alias does the same thing as the full command does.

The fourth chapter of the book focuses on the input and output of Linux commands. There are some standard outputs, inputs, and some errors. To start with, I will explain what standard error is and how it is displayed. The next section focuses on the standard output and the error in a single file. In the next section, I will shed light on what standard input is. Linux pipelines are also very important when it comes to operating a Linux shell.

The fifth chapter of the book deals in-depth with the Linux shell. I will explain the different features of the shell, such as the Tilde expansion and the arithmetic involved in the Linux operating system. I will explain the importance of double quotes in Linux. You will also learn about the importance of escaping characters and their role in the Linux operating system. If you are not a keyboard lover, you will not enjoy Linux. Linux is about using the keyboard. Therefore, you should know about some amazing tricks for using the keyboard fast and efficiently. I will conclude the chapter by explaining some a bunch of keyboard shortcuts.

The sixth chapter of the book focuses on the configuration and Linux environment. In the first section, I will keep my focus on the environment variables, which are USER, SHELL, HOME, LANG, and DISPLAY, etc. You will know what each variable is capable of and how you can use them in your day to day Linux operations. The next section contains the details on how you can easily establish the Linux environment. Linux editors are very important if you want to be a pro in Linux usage. If you know other computer languages such as Python, you will not be surprised by hearing about text editors. As shell scripting is almost like coding a program, you will love to go through this section that will introduce you to a bunch of text editors. I will give details about the top editors before moving on to giving a comprehensive note on the most famous editor, namely *vi.* You can download it and install it on your system to edit shell scripts. You can customize your shell prompt, and I will explain in the next section. You also can add colors to your interface by applying some keyboard codes like CTRL-D or CTRL-F. You will be able to scan the real codes in the chapter itself. There is a way to move the cursor in a really fast manner with some amazing keyboard hacks. I will give details about the hacks, and you will enjoy it.

The seventh chapter of the book focuses on writing shell scripts. In this chapter, I will explain how to write a script, format it, and create a script file. So, this chapter provides a launching pad for you to learn scriptwriting in Linux.

The eighth chapter sheds light on the structured commands. The first on the line is the if-then statement. This is the decision-making process of the shell. You can apply the script to make some simple mathematical calculations. You also can use the statements to explore the files stored on the system. I will give you practical applications of the conditionals. You can take the script and paste it in a text editor to see the execution. Edit it and change it as per your desire to learn the in-depth application. I will explain the importance of double parenthesis while you do mathematical calculations.

In the next section, I will explain how a *for* command can be used in scriptwriting to do some amazing tricks. The basic job of a for loop is the same in shell scripting as in other languages, iteration through lists, strings, or other loops. I will explain in the next section the ins and outs of the while loop. This is one of the most interesting sections of the book. The while loop will help you add the return value in the script. You can make sure that the loop iterates through the script as long as a certain condition is true. You can add multiple while loops in a single script, which makes complex programming easier and fun. The next on the line is the 'until loop. This loop has a similar structure as that of the while loop. The next section is one of the most interesting ones in this chapter. In this section, I will explain what nesting loops are and how you can nest one loop into another one. I will explain the method of nesting one for loop into another. Afterward, we will look at nesting a for loop into a while loop and an until loop into a while loop.

The next section of the chapter carries details on how you can use the break command. The break command breaks a loop at the point you want it to and terminates the loop. I have given a few examples to explain how you can integrate the break command in the Linux shell loops. The next two sections are linked to the break command. A Linux shell script contains more than one loops at times. Some loops are the outer loops, while others are named the inner loops. When you integrate the break command in the loops, you can specify the position to terminate the loop that you need to.

The termination of one loop does not affect the run of the other loop. I will further explain the topics with relevant examples.

Coupled with the break command is the continue command. There is a slight nuance between the two commands. While the break command tends to break the script and terminate the loop, the continue command breaks the loop at the point you specify in the script but restarts the loop at another point. See the example in the section to understand how you can integrate a continue command in Linux shell script.

Next comes the case command. The chapter ends on a comprehensive discussion on Linux shell functions. Linux functions a bit similar to Python functions. You have to define a function first, and then you can use it later on in the script by making a function call. There is no need to rewrite lengthy blocks of code in the script. So, you can say that functions save you time.

The second last chapter of the book deals with adding colors to the script. In this section, I will educate you on how to create menus in Linux. Linux is different from Windows in the sense that it allows the user to customize menus and interface in general. While this sounds fun, this is a bit tricky as well. You will have to learn the script needed to make a creative design for your main menu or your interface in general. You will have to brainstorm on the right colors for the design. This chapter has the needed knowledge to accomplish this. You will learn about creating a menu and adding colors to it by using the right color codes.

The last chapter of the book is a brief one as it contains scripts for creating programs in Linux. I will build a script for a simple calculator that would do the four basic mathematical operations for you. You can take the code and alter the positions of the operators or add more operators as per need. Execute the script in the shell and see how it works.

Who Should Read This Book?

This book is for everyone who wants the basic knowhow about Linux. The people who have the basic knowledge can use this book to create some interesting things like writing shell scripts and creating programs. This book is the best way to learn about Linux administration. You do not have to be the base knowledge to go through this book. Even if you are not aiming at learning pure coding, you can use this book to learn about the basic Linux shell commands. This book should be the hot favorite of those people who are looking forward to switching from the Windows operating system to the Linux operating system. Have a happy and joyful read.

Chapter One

What Is Linux?

L inux is an operating system just like a Windows operating system. An operating system is a software layer that lies between the hardware of the system and you. An operating system allows you to do different types of things on a computer, such as composing a document, designing, or coding a program. An operating system allows the software to communicate with the hardware. For example, when you ask the computer to print a specific page, it is the operating system that plays the role of a missing link between the software and the hardware.

Similarly, you can store information on hard drives with the help of the operating system. Linux is an operating system that helps you form the connection. It acts as a bridge between your instructions and the physical devices you have connected to your computer system. The main thing that you must realize is that the software that you will run on it will be of a different type as compared to the one which you usually run on a Windows operating system. Desktop apps such as Adobe Photoshop ad Microsoft Office are not compatible with a Linux environment. Linux usually runs servers such as web virtualization servers, Apache web servers, and database servers.

However, there are a few Linux distributions that are specifically made for desktop computers and are quite similar to Mac OS and Windows in the sense that they run photo editing and video editing programs, which usually Windows operating systems run. You also can install and run games, web browsing applications, program development applications, and all other programs that are specific to Windows operating systems.

Linux started as a kernel, which is created by Linus Torvalds during his student life at the University of Helsinki. A Linux kernel is the defining component of the Linux operating system. It is responsible for interfacing all applications to the physical hardware. Between 1991 and 1994, Linus Trivolds combined Linux kernel with GNU OS to create a Linux operating system. He wanted an operating system as something which he could customize as per his programming needs.

At first glance, Linux seems to be pretty much complicated. Several pieces run simultaneously and communicate that way too. A web server will appear to be talking to a database server that would be using a shared library that other programs might also be using at the same time. The top effective way to understand how Linux or any other operating system works is through the method of abstraction. This is a fancy way of saying that you can just ignore what was happening in the background. Take the example of a bus. When you ride it, you do not pay attention to most of the details that are happening around you. You do not think about mounting bolts that are holding the motor inside of the structure of the bus. You also don't consider the people who built the bus for you to drive or the road you travel to your destination. The main idea that you have about the bus is that you are riding it and it is taking you to your destination. As a rider, this information is more than enough, but as a driver of the bus, you need more information. You must learn how to operate the steering wheel, the peddles, and the gear. If you are having a rough ride on the bus, the abstraction of the bus can be divided into three parts; the first bus itself, the road, and your driving skills. You cannot blame the bus if the road is bumpy or your driving skills are poor. Software developers use abstraction as a tool when they are building some kind of operating system and its applications. There are lots of terms for the abstracted subdivision in computer software such as modules, subsystems, and packages. Let us take a look at some components of the Linux system.

Abstraction Layers in Linux

If you use abstraction for splitting up the computing systems into different components, you can make things easier for you to understand. Still, it needs to work in a proper organization. Components ought to be arranged into layers. A layer in a Linux operating system is the classification of where a specific component sits in between a user and hardware. Components like web browsers and games secure the top layer of Linux while the memory of the system sits at the bottom. Memory is in the form of 0s and 1s. In between, the operating system occupies most of the layers.

A Linux system has three major levels. The hardware sits at the base; it includes the memory of the system and one or multiple

Central Processing Units (CPUs) to perform the computation work and also to read from as well as write to the memory. Network interfaces and disks are also considered parts of the hardware.

The next level is the kernel, which forms the core of your operating system. A kernel is a software that resides in the memory that instructs the CPU what it ought to do. The kernel generally manages hardware parts of the system, and it also acts as an interface between a running system and the hardware.

There are certain processes always running in Linux. These processes are generally running programs that the kernel has been managing. Collectively, they make up the upper level of the system, which is known as the userspace. More specifically, they are known as a user process. All web servers are called user processes.

There is a visible difference between the ways how user processes and kernel run. The kernel usually runs in the kernel-mode while user processes run in the user mode. The code that runs through in the kernel-mode has unrestricted access to the main memory and the processor, dubbed as a robust yet lethal privilege that permits a kernel to crash the system. The area which the only kernel has access to is dubbed as kernel space.

Userspace is the part of the main memory of the system which the user processes have access to. A user process that goes off the track can cause some serious damage to the system.

System Hardware

Of all the hardware on a computer system, the main memory is the most important part of the system. In the rawest form, the main memory is like a big storage area to keep up information in the form of 0s and 1s. Each 0 or 1 is a bit. Kernel and the processes reside in the main memory and store enormous collections of bits. The input and output from the peripheral devices flow through the main system memory in the form of bits. The CPU read data from memory. As for a new term state, it is used regarding the memory, kernel, and the processes of your computer system. Simply put, a state is a specific arrangement of bits. If you have four bits stored in the memory 0110, 1011, and 0001 are three different states.

The Kernel

Everything the kernel does is related to the main category. One of its main tasks is splitting of memory into a wide range of subdivisions. It ought to maintain state information on the subdivisions. Each process has its share of memory. The kernel needs to ensure that each process keeps its share.

- The kernel determines which processes are permitted to use the CPU and which are not.

- It keeps track of the memory of the system, which different processes share.

- The kernel works as an interface between processes and hardware of the system, such as hard disk drives. It operates the hardware.

User Spaces

As I have mentioned earlier, the main memory of the system which the kernel allocates to users is dubbed as userspace. Userspace also refers to the memory for all running processes. The most real action happens in the userspace. Each process performs a different function for the user.

Chapter Two

Linux Commands

Linux shell is also known as the Linux command line. The shell is generally a program which receives keyboard commands and transmits them to the operating system for execution. It is the medium between you and the operating system. All Linux distributions have a shell program known as bash, the short form of Bourne Again Shell. When you are using a graphical interface for Linux, you need some other program known as the terminal emulator. This can help you interact with the shell.

The First Keys

The first step is to launch the terminal emulator. Once it pops up, you can see something like the following:

[mak567@localhost ~]$

If you see the $ sign in place of #, you are logged in as a regular user. The # sign shows that you are logged in as the root or superuser. This is the shell prompt, and it shows up every time the shell is perfectly ready for accepting input. The appearance may vary based on the distribution, but its function will always be the same. You can see it like this: username@machinename. It means you can change the names as per your requirements. If you type in the prompt some random alphabets, it will return the result, which

17

would make no sense at all. The shell tells that the command cannot be found, and then it once again shows the prompt so that you can type some other thing and get the result.

[mak567@localhost ~]$ sjkhksjdhfhh

sh: sjkhksjdhfhh: not found

You can check the command history by pressing the up-arrow key; the history will appear at the prompt. Linux distributions can remember up to 500 commands as per their default setting. When you press the down arrow, the previous command will disappear. As you can recall the previous command with the up-arrow, you can position the cursor by using the right-left arrow keys. This makes editing the line of code easier and less tough. You can move the right and left arrow keys and add or erase any words or alphabets that you have mistakenly entered.

Mouse

The shell or the command line is all about expertly using the keyboard. However, if you are not comfortable with that, you can use a mouse with the terminal emulator. There is a built-in mechanism in the X Window System. You can perform a copy and paste function by using a mouse.

The Shell Window

When you have logged in on your operating system, you need to open the shell window or the Linux terminal. Once you have done that, it will display a prompt. Let's try some commands to see how the shell behaves.

> [mak567@localhost ~]$ echo Hello, I am trying to learn Lin ux administration.

Hello, I am trying to learn Linux administration.

Now I will use the cat command to display the content of the passwd file. The file usually contains system information. Let's try it.

> [mak567@localhost ~]$ cat /etc/passwd
>
> root:x:0:0:root:/root:/bin/sh
>
> daemon:x:1:1:daemon:/usr/sbin:/bin/false
>
> bin:x:2:2:bin:/bin:/bin/false
>
> sys:x:3:3:sys:/dev:/bin/false

Basic Shell Commands

The first one on the line is the ls command that will display the contents of a directory in the form of a list. The default is the current directory. You can use ls -1 for a detailed listing. You can use ls –F for displaying the file type information. Before delving deeper into all the above-mentioned complex commands, let's start with the simplest commands. You can check the free space on your disk by the following command. Just type df in the shell.

> [mak567@localhost ~]$ df

```
Filesystem        1K-
blocks      Used Available Use% Mounted on
/dev/root         1048576   454620   593956  43% /
devtmpfs            61068        0    61068   0% /dev
tmpfs               61224        0    61224   0% /run
```

You also can check how much memory is currently free in your computer system the command needed for the purpose is 'free.'

```
[mak567@localhost ~]$ free
              total    used     free   shared  buffers   cached
Mem:        122448     5192   117256        0        0      468
-/+ buffers/cache:      4724   117724
Swap:            0        0        0
```

If you desire to end a terminal session, simply write exit in the shell, and you will be immediately out of the system.

Exploring the File System

There is a hierarchical directory structure system. All the files are organized in a tree-like pattern of directories that are called folders in the Windows operating system. The very first directory in the Linux file system is commonly known as the root directory. It contains different files and a wide range of sub-directories and so on. Linux is different from windows in the sense that it has a unified filesystem tree. It doesn't matter how many drives and storage devices you have linked to the system; they will be displayed in the form of a single file system tree. Unlike Windows, there are no pictures of a tree system but a maze. You can see the pathway to the file, known as the parent directory. The directory in which you are working is known as the working directory. You can use the pwd command to see in which directory you are in.

[mak567@localhost ~]$ pwd

/home/mak567

You can specify the directory in which you want to work, just like the following.

[mak567@localhost ~]$ ls /usr

bin   libexec

i486-buildroot-linux-uclibc local

include   sbin

lib   share

lib32   var

lib64

There is a command by which you can specify multiple directories by a single attempt. I will use the same command, but after adding a new character ~ in it.

[mak567@localhost ~]$ ls ~ /usr

/home/mak567:

/usr:

bin   libexec

i486-buildroot-linux-uclibc local

include   sbin

lib   share

lib32   var

lib64

The shell displayed both directories one by one.

The command ls –1 will display the longer version of the list of a directory. You also can reverse the order in which the shell has displayed the list. For the purpose, you will have to add --reverse to the end of the same command just like the following:

[mak567@localhost ~]$ ls -1 --reverse

ls: unrecognized option `--reverse'

BusyBox v1.24.2 (2019-04-14 15:55:47 CEST) multi-call binary.

Usage: ls [-1AaCxdLHRFplinsehrSXvctu] [-w WIDTH] [FILE]...

List directory contents

       -1   One column output

       -a   Include entries which start with .

       -A   Like -a, but exclude . and ..

       -C   List by columns

-x   List by lines

-d   List directory entries instead of contents

You will have the display as per your Linux system. You can use the –all command to display the total number of files with names that would start with a period.

[mak567@localhost ~]$ ls -all

total 12

drwx------   3 mak567   input   61 May 2 15:54 .

drwxr-xr-x   3 root   root   60 May 24 2017 ..

drwx------

    2 mak567   input   90 May 2 15:54 .vfsync

There is an option '--directory,' which will specify the directory that you are trying to display. It will find the directory and list its contents but not the directory itself. You can use the same option in combination with the -l option to unearth the details about the directory instead of its contents. The –l command alludes to the longer version of the content you are trying to display in the shell. The third option is –F, which can also be written as –human-readable. It will display long-form listings that, too, in a human-readable format by nearly displaying the names instead of bytes. The –S command in the shell will sort out the lists for you by the size of the files while –t will sort out the files regarding the modification time of the files.

Determining A File's Type

Linux allows you to check which file is of what type. If you are a Windows user, you might be aware of the fact that it is quite a hassle to confirm which file type you are using. Filenames in Linux are not generally required to reflect the content of the file. In Windows operating system, you have to put videos in the videos folder and pictures in the pictures folder. For the pictures, you will have to use the extension jpg. All this is done for the sake of easy identification of files and their contents. That's not the case in Linux. You can invoke the file you need by the following command.

[mak567@localhost ~]$ file images.jpg

You will be able to see the type of content that is in the folder. You will also see in which form the content rests in the folder. There are different types of files that you will have to deal with during your work. Scan them with the help of this command.

View Content

Linux gives you a simple command to view text files that sit on your system, which is the 'less' command. All through your Linux system, there are lots of files that carry human-readable text. You can easily examine all content of your files. You can open up the files that contain the settings of your system, known as configuration files. Using this command, you can convert them into a human-readable format and scan them to understand how your operating system works. Many of the real programs that the system uses are also stored in the same format.

Generally, there are lots of ways to represent information on a computer system. All these methods involve defining a relationship between the information and a bunch of numbers used to represent the same. Computers consider and understand each snippet of information in the form of numbers. Therefore, they convert each type of data into a numeric representation. Some of the representations are complex such as videos, while others are simple such as word files. Linux stores lots of data in the text format, and there are lots of Linux tools that work with text files. Coming back to the less command, you can use the same in the following manner.

[mak567@localhost ~]$ less /etc/passwd

The /etc/passwd is the name and path of the file I want to explore. You can enter the filename that you need to explore. Give it a try by picking up some random filename from your computer and type it in the shell. Once the command kicks off the program, you can view the contents. If the file is a long one, you can scroll up and down. When you want to close it, just enter the Q key.

Note: When you are in the less program, you can use Page Up and Down to scroll up and down. You can use Page Down + Spacebar to scroll forward by one page. The Up and Down arrows can be used to scroll up and down a single line. G is used to move to the end of the file. Use 'n' to search for the next occurrence of your previous search while use h to display the help screen. Similarly, use 1G or simply g to move up to the start of the text file.

Some Random Commands

Linux is very interesting if you are knowledgeable about the commands that the shell accepts. The right commands will speed up the processes of the Linux shell system.

- The command /bin will display the binaries that should be present in a Linux system if you want it to boot and run smoothly.

- The command /boot will lead you to the Linux kernel. It will also lead you to an initial RAM disk image and the boot loader.

- The command /etc. opens a directory that contains configuration files of the system. In addition to this, it also contains a bunch of shell scripts that would start the system services at boot time. Everything that exists in the directory ought to be a readable text.

- The command /dev is a special directory that possesses device nodes.

- The command /home allows the users to write files in the home directory.

- The command /lib contains a shared library that the core system programs use. They are quite similar to DLLs in the Windows Operating system.

The ls Command

The ls command generally lists different contents of a directory of your Linux operating system. The default is your current directory. You can use ls –l to display a longer version of the same directory. The command ls –l will help you display the information about the file type. You can type them in the shell in the following manner.

```
[mak567@localhost ~]$ ls

[mak567@localhost ~]$ ls -1

[mak567@localhost ~]$ ls –F

[mak567@localhost ~]$ ls

goof  pic

[mak567@localhost ~]$ mkdir books

[mak567@localhost ~]$ mkdir glasses

[mak567@localhost ~]$ mkdir software

[mak567@localhost ~]$ mkdir python

[mak567@localhost ~]$ mkdir watches

[mak567@localhost ~]$ mkdir videos

[mak567@localhost ~]$ ls

books  glasses  goof  pic  python  software  videos  watches
```

You can see that I had only two directories at the start. Then I added more directories with the mkdir command, and afterward, I used the ls command to see the details. The ls command revealed the details of the home directory. The addition of -1 to the ls command will display the content in the long-form while the addition of –F will display file type information.

[mak567@localhost ~]$ ls -1

books

glasses

goof

pic

python

software

videos

watches

[mak567@localhost ~]$ ls -F

books/ glasses/ goof/ pic/ python/ software/ videos/ watches

/

The cp Command

If you want to use it in its simplest form, cp means copying files. For example, you have two files, namely zen1 and zen2. If you want to copy the first to the second, you can use the cp command in the following way.

[mak567@localhost ~]$ cp zen1 zen2

If you want to copy multiple files to a directory, you can try the following method. I have three files, namely zen1, zen2, and zen3, and I want to copy all of them to a directory named goof, I will write the command like the following.

[mak567@localhost ~]$ zen1 zen2 zen3 goof

You should keep in mind that directories in Linux are the same thing as folders in Windows operating system.

The touch Command

There is another interesting command in Linux, known as the touch command. If the file exists on the system, the touch command will not affect it, but it will update the modification time of the file. You can create an empty file by the following command.

[mak567@localhost ~]$ touch zen1

Zen1 is the name of the file. Now run ls –l on the same file. You will be able to see the date and time of the moment you ran the touch command on the same file.

[mak567@localhost ~]$ touch zen1

[mak567@localhost ~]$ ls -l

total 0

-rw-r--r-- 1 mak567 input 0 May 4 16:21 zen1

The mv Command

The mv (move) command behaves just like the cp command. It can rename a specific file. For example, it can rename zen1 to zen2. Let's see how it works.

[mak567@localhost ~]$ mv zen1 zen2

Navigating Different Directories

A Linux shell runs on a hierarchy of directories that are displayed as '/' and are sometimes named the root directory. The separator of each directory in the hierarchy is '/.' Do not use the backslash. There are many subdirectories inside the root directory. When you refer to a directory or a file, you need to specify a pathname or a path. A path starts with '/.' It is considered a full or absolute path.

The cd command refers to the current working directory. The cd command attempts to change the current working directory of the shell. If you eliminate dir from the code, the shell will push you back to the home directory, the directory you had started in, and where you logged in at the start.

[mak567@localhost ~]$ cd dir

The next command is known as mkdir, which creates a brand new directory for your usage.

[mak567@localhost ~]$ mkdir pics

Another command known as the rmdir command tends to delete the directory named pics.

[mak567@localhost ~]$ mkdir apple

[mak567@localhost ~]$ rmdir apple

[mak567@localhost ~]$ cd apple

/bin/sh: cd: can't cd to apple

[mak567@localhost ~]$ mkdir apple

[mak567@localhost ~]$ cd apple

[mak567@localhost apple]$ cd

[mak567@localhost ~]$ rmdir apple

[mak567@localhost ~]$ cd apple

/bin/sh: cd: can't cd to apple

The grep command tends to print different lines from a single file or an input stream that matches an expression. If you want to print the lines in the /etc/passwd file that also contains the text root, you need to enter the following:

[mak567@localhost ~]$ grep root /etc/passwd

The grep command is quite extraordinarily handy when it comes to operating on multiple files because it will print the filename and other details. In case you want to check all files in /etc which contains the word root, you can use the following command.

[mak567@localhost ~]$ grep root /etc/*

The less Command

The less command is very helpful when you come across a file that is very big or when the output of a command is long, and you have to scroll off the screen. When you apply the less command, you will see that the contents of a file on an on the space of a single screen. You need to press the spacebar to move forward and the b key to skip a screenful of content to the back. If you want to quit the command, type q in the shell. The less command is considered as an enhanced version of a program named as more. Most of the Linux servers and desktops offer less command, but it is generally not considered as standard on many embedded systems. If you can't use the less command, you can try more. You also can search for pieces of text inside less.

The rm Command

```
[mak567@localhost books]$ cd books

/bin/sh: cd: can't cd to books

[mak567@localhost books]$ cd

[mak567@localhost ~]$ cd books

[mak567@localhost books]$ cd

[mak567@localhost ~]$ cd goof

[mak567@localhost goof]$ cd

[mak567@localhost ~]$ cd python

[mak567@localhost python]$ cd
```

```
[mak567@localhost ~]$ cd software

[mak567@localhost software]$ cd

[mak567@localhost ~]$ cd watches

[mak567@localhost watches]$ cd

[mak567@localhost ~]$ cd pic

[mak567@localhost pic]$ cd

[mak567@localhost ~]$ rmdir books

 [mak567@localhost ~]$ rmdir python

[mak567@localhost ~]$ rmdir software

[mak567@localhost ~]$ rmdir watches

[mak567@localhost ~]$ cd books

/bin/sh: cd: can't cd to books

[mak567@localhost ~]$ cd python

/bin/sh: cd: can't cd to python

[mak567@localhost ~]$ cd software

/bin/sh: cd: can't cd to software

[mak567@localhost ~]$ cd watches

/bin/sh: cd: can't cd to watches
```

You can see that the rmdir command has removed all the directories that I mentioned. You can use the rm –rf command to permanently delete a directory from the Linux system along with its contents, but you ought to be careful. This is one of the commands that have the potential to inflict serious damage to your system. The –r option triggers a recursive delete strategy to delete different things in a repeated manner.

Change Your Password

You can use the passwd command to change the password. You will be asked for the old password first, and then you will be prompted to enter the new password twice in the shell. You can choose a password that does not have any real words or language. Never try to combine different words while creating a password. One of the easiest ways is creating a password by picking a sentence that would be an acronym. You can then add a comma or any other punctuation mark to the acronym. Then just remember the sentence. You can change the shell by using the chsh command.

The ln Command

The ln command is generally used for hard and symbolic links. You can use it in the following formats.

    [mak567@local ~]$ ln file link

To create a hard link, you can use the following code.

    [mak567@local ~]$ ln –s item link

Hard links generally are original Unix way of forming links. Symbolic links are modern.

Chapter Three

Being Practical with Commands

L inux is rich with commands which you can use to get things done fast and in the way you like. There is a series of mysterious commands, each having its mysterious options as well as arguments. In this chapter, I will shed light on how to work with Linux commands and how you can create your commands as well.

Defining Commands

A command can be an executable program, just all the files in different directories. Executable programs are also known as compiled binaries like the ones that are written in C++ and C. They also are the programs that are usually written in the form of a scripting language such as shell, Ruby, Python, Perl, etc.

Several commands are shell builtins. For example, the cd command that you have read about in the past chapters is a shell builtin. Then there is shell function, which is a miniature shell script properly incorporated in the environment. The alias command is the one that you build yourself as per your requirements.

Unveil Commands

It is quite an interesting thing concerning commands. You can use the type command in the shell to unveil the type of command which you are using. This is helpful if you are a newbie to the world of Linux. You can just enter the command and know what the purpose of different shell commands is. Let's see how it works. In the following code example, I will enter different commands along with the type of command to know what they are exactly.

```
[mak567@localhost ~]$ type cd

cd is a shell builtin

[mak567@localhost ~]$ type type

type is a shell builtin

[mak567@localhost ~]$ type ls

ls is /bin/ls

[mak567@localhost ~]$ type cp

cp is /bin/cp

[mak567@localhost ~]$ type rm

rm is /bin/rm

[mak567@localhost ~]$ type mkdir

mkdir is /bin/mkdir

[mak567@localhost ~]$ type passwd

passwd is /usr/bin/passwd

[mak567@localhost ~]$ type more

more is /bin/more
```

So, if at any point you want to know whether a command is a built-in or not, you can use the type command to know what it is and how it will work.

The which Command

Linux, unlike Windows operating systems, often has more than a single version of an executable program. If you want to determine the exact location of the executable program, you can use the *which* command.

[mak567@localhost ~]$ which ls

/bin/ls

[mak567@localhost ~]$ which cd

[mak567@localhost ~]$ which rm

/bin/rm

[mak567@localhost ~]$ which mkdir

/bin/mkdir

[mak567@localhost ~]$ which cp

/bin/cp

[mak567@localhost ~]$ which passwd

/usr/bin/passwd

[mak567@localhost ~]$ which more

/bin/more

[mak567@localhost ~]$ which less

/usr/bin/less

The difference you might have noted in the above commands is that the 'which' command didn't work on the 'cd,' which is a built-in command. The takeaway is that the which command doesn't affect any built-in command. Either it will show an error message, or it will simply pass on as it did in the shell when I paired it up with the cd command. Passing on is a polite way of saying 'command not found in the system.'

Documentation of a Command

The first command on the line is the help command that can get help for the built-in commands of the shell. You can type help in the shell and the name of the built-in command and see the documentation about the command.

[mak567@localhost ~]$ help cd

The man Command

Most of the executable programs are usually intended for command-line use, and they generally come with a man page or manual. The page also called man has information for the user to view. You can type man followed by the name of the program to see what is in the manual. Man pages vary concerning format, but in general, they carry a title and a synopsis of the command. It will tell you what the purpose of the command is. It will also tell you about the listing and the description of the different options of the command. A lot of pages include examples that are intended as a reference. You can enter this command in the shell in the following format.

[mak567@localhost ~]$ man ls

On a majority of the Linux operating systems, the man command uses 'less' to show the manual page. The manual is generally broken into small sections, and it covers a wide range of things such as programming interfaces, admin commands, and file formats, etc. It may happen at times that you need to look into a specific section of the manual to find out what you are looking for.

The apropos Command

It is possible to search the list of different man pages for possible matches that are based on the search term.

[mak567@localhost ~]$ apropos floppy

The whatis Command

The whatis program tends to display the full name along with one-line info of a man page.

[mak567@localhost ~]$ whatis ls

info

The manual pages are not reader-friendly. These pages are generally supplied with Unix and Linux terms, which are quite frustrating to comprehend. You can use them as reference documentation but not something as a tutorial to understand the purpose of each command. Therefore you can use the GNU Project as an alternative option. The project contains info pages which are generally displayed as reader-oriented program dubbed as 'info.'

These pages are hyperlinked like web pages. This program has one job to read info files, which are in the form of tree-like structures. Each node of the tree contains a single topic. These files contain hyperlinks that move from node to node. You can identify a hyperlink by an asterisk. You can activate it by putting the cursor on it and by pressing the ENTER key.

- Use ? to display the command help.

- You can use BACKSPACE or PAGE UP to display the previous page of information.

- You can use Spacebar or PAGE DOWN to display the next page of information.

- Type u to display the parent node of what you are viewing right now.

- Type n to move on to the next node of the file tree.

- Type p to view the previous node of the file tree.

- Type ENTER any instant to follow the hyperlink at the location of the cursor.

- Type q any time to quit the program.

Most of the programs are usually part of the GNU Project's coreutils package. You can find more details about it by the following command.

```
[mak567@localhost ~]$ info coreutils
```

It will display a menu page that contains hyperlinks to the documentation of each program, which is provided by the coreutils package.

Is There a Readme?

There are lots of software packages on your system that usually have documentation files inside of the /usr/share/doc directory. Many of them are generally stored in a plaintext format, and they can be viewed with the help of a web browser. You may see some files with a .gz extension. This means that the files are in the compressed format.

Creating a Command With Alias

In the following example, you will be able to experience first-hand programming in Linux. You will create your command by using the alias command. Before you start, you need to reveal a small command-line known as a trick. Also, it is quite possible to put one command on a single line by separating each part with the ; character. Let's see how it works.

```
[mak567@localhost ~]$ com1; com2; com3
```

Take a look at the example.

```
[mak567@localhost ~]$ cd /usr; ls; cd -

bin                     libexec

i486-buildroot-linux-uclibc  local
```

include   sbin

lib   share

lib32   var

lib64

/home/mak567

In this example, three commands have been combined on the first line. In the first command, I changed the directory to /usr. Then I listed the directory, and then finally, I returned to the original directory by using the cd - command. This is how I got back to where I had started. Let's repeat the sequence by turning it into a new command with the help of using an alias. The very first is to carve out a name for the command. Make sure that the name you carve-out is not already in use by the Linux system. Thankfully, we have the 'type' command to check if the file of a particular name already exists in the system or not. Let's see how to do that.

[mak567@localhost ~]$ type goof

goof: not found

The file name goof doesn't exist in the system; therefore, you can use it as your alias. You also can check for other filenames as suit your taste and requirement.

[mak567@localhost ~]$ alias goof='cd /usr; ls; cd -'

Now the alias command has been created. After writing the alias, I wrote the name goof and then moved on to writing the equal sign, followed by a quoted string that contained the code, meaning to be assigned to a name. After the alias has been defined, you can use it anywhere in the shell.

[mak567@localhost ~]$ goof

bin   libexec

i486-buildroot-linux-uclibc local

include   sbin

lib   share

lib32   var

lib64

/home/mak567

You can see that the alias command did the same thing that the original command did. You can also check the status of the alias command, like to which command it has been associated.

[mak567@localhost ~]$ type goof

goof is an alias for cd /usr; ls; cd -

If any point during operating Linux, you need to remove the alias from the shell, you can just unalias it. Follow the underneath code to undo what you did earlier.

[mak567@localhost ~]$ unalias goof

[mak567@localhost ~]$ type goof

goof: not found

In the above example, I purposely avoided naming the alias to an existing file. However, in some cases, it becomes necessary to do so. If you want to see how many aliases exist in the system, simply write alias in the system, and you will have a list of all the existing ones.

[mak567@localhost ~]$ alias

goof='cd /usr; ls; cd -'

As I have only one alias in the system, my system shows the same.

Chapter Four

Input/Output

The input and output in the shell can be redirected from one file to another. You also can connect a set of commands to create robust command pipelines. Several commands come under the umbrella of I/O redirection. You might have used lots of programs that produce a standard output of one or the other kind. The output generally is of two types. The first one is about the result of a program, which is the data a program is created to produce. The second one is about the error messages or the status messages which tell you what is wrong with a program or how the program is running. Simple commands like ls display their results and the error messages they contain. The I/O redirection is about redefining where the standard output will go. You can redirect it to another file instead of letting it pop up on the screen. You can use the > operator to do the job. The reason as to why you want to do this is that it is quite beneficial to store the output of this command inside of a single file. You can tell the shell to channelize the output of the ls command to ls-otpt.txt instead of your screen.

[mak567@localhost ~]$ ls -l /usr/bin > ls-otpt.txt

[mak567@localhost ~]$ ls -l ls-otpt.txt

-rw-r--r-- 1 mak567 input   26123 May 5 16:32 ls-otpt.txt

You can see that the output of the file has been redirected to the text file named ls-otpt.txt. To see the output of the command, I had to invoke the file and open it in the shell. In the next phase, I will repeat the same redirection test but in a different way. This time I will change the directory's name to the one that doesn't exist.

[mak567@localhost ~]$ ls -l /usr/beef > ls-otpt.txt

ls: /usr/beef: No such file or directory

As the beef directory doesn't exist in the system, what I got was an error message. The error message jumped to the shell screen instead of moving on into the text file that I mentioned in the code. The problem is that the ls command doesn't allow its error messages to travel into a text file. Moreover, we redirected only the standard output and not the standard error. Linux takes standard output as different from a standard error. Let's see how to redirect a standard error.

Standard Error

If you are looking forward to redirecting a standard error, you must refer to the file descriptor. A standard program can produce an output of multiple numbered file streams. You can use three file descriptors such as 0, 1, and 2. You can redirect the standard error with the following notation.

[mak567@localhost ~]$ ls -l /usr/beef 2> file name

The file descriptor 2 is generally placed before the operator for redirection. The standard error will be redirected to the respected file.

Output and Error in One File

Suppose you wish to capture the output as well as the error to a single file. In that case, you need to redirect the standard output and the standard error to a single file. Generally, there are two ways to execute this. The first is the traditional way, which works with the older versions of Linux shell.

[mak567@localhost ~]$ ls -l /usr/beef > ls-otpt.txt 2>&1

With the help of this method, you can perform two redirections in a single attempt. In the first phase, the standard output of a command is redirected to the file ls-otpt.txt, and then the file descriptor 2, which is for standard error, has been redirected to the descriptor 1, which is for standard output. The notation 2>&1 did the magic for us. The important thing to note down is that the redirections' order is important. The redirection must always happen after redirecting the standard output, or it will not work.

Linux offers you a chance to discard the unwanted output. It is sometimes in the best interest of the Linux administrator to do away with the extra talking on the screen. You can throw it in the trash can. You can do the same with the error messages and the status messages as well. The Linux system usually offers a way to do the same by letting you redirect the output to a specific file /dev/null. This file acts as a bit bucket for the Linux system that accepts the input but does nothing with it. You can apply the following command to suppress certain error messages. Let's see how to do that.

[mak567@localhost ~]$ ls -l /usr/beef 2> /dev/null

The bit bucket is one of the ancient Unix concepts. If someone says that he or she is sending your comments to dev null, you should understand what it means.

Standard Input

Just like standard output and standard error, you can redirect standard input as well. The first method to do this is by using the cat command. The cat command usually is used to concatenate a set of files. It takes one or more files, reads them, and copies them to display in the standard output. You can consider 'cat' as something analogous to the TYPE command in MS-DOS. Use it in the following manner.

[mak567@localhost ~]$ cat ls-output.txt

This command will display the file ls-output.txt and is used to display different short text files. You also can use cat command independently with no additional arguments. So, what happens if you enter the cat command without any arguments?

[mak567@localhost ~]$ ls cat

Usually, nothing happens. It sits without any action. If you don't give any arguments to the 'cat,' it generally reads from the standard input. Since standard input is linked to the keyboard, you need to type something so that the cat command reads it.

[mak567@localhost ~]$ cat

I am learning Linux administration faster than other students.

I am learning Linux administration faster than other students.

To break free from the standard input loop, you will need to enter Ctrl + d. Upon entering the same, you will be able to see the shell prompt. If you create a file, namely linuxlearning.txt and desire to send the output to the same, you can write the following command in the shell.

[mak567@localhost ~]$ cat > linuxlearning.txt

I am learning Linux administration faster than other students.

By using the redirection operator, you can change the source of standard output to the file linuxlearning.txt. The result is the same as the previous command, but this is not useful as compared to passing a filename argument. Other commands make good use of the standard input.

Linux Pipelines

The tendency of commands to read data from a bunch of standard input and then redirect it to standard output is generally utilized by a special shell feature, namely pipelines. By using the pipe operator, you can forward the standard output of one command to the standard input of another command. To complete this action, you are going to need a bunch of commands. You can use 'less' to display the output of any command that sends its results to standard output. By using the technique, you can examine the output of any command that tends to produce standard output.

[mak567@localhost ~]$ ls –l /usr/bin | less

Pipelines are more often used to perform some complex operations on the data. It is quite possible to put multiple commands together in a single pipeline. The commands use this way as filters. Filter, in the Linux operating system, take the input, alter it, and then display the output in a matter of seconds. Just imagine you need to make a combined list of a bunch of executable programs in /bin and in /usr/bin. Try to put all of them in a sorted form and then view the list.

[mak567@localhost ~]$ ls /bin /usr/bin | sort | less

You might have noticed that I specified two directories in the command. The output of ls has two sorted lines, one for each directory. By including sort in the pipeline, you can change the data to yield one sorted list.

There is a special command in Linux, well-known as the uniq command. It is often used in conjunction with the sort command. The uniq command accepts data that has been sorted. The data may come from either standard input or a single filename argument. It also, by default, removes any kind of duplicates from your list. To make sure that you have no duplicates, you ought to remove them from the list. Duplicates generally refer to the programs that tend to pop up in the /bin and /usr/bin directories. Here is how you can add uniq to your pipeline.

[mak567@localhost ~]$ ls /bin /usr/bin | sort | uniq | less

Let's see how you can remove any duplicates from the output of the sort command. If you want to see the list of duplicates, you can add -d to uniq.

The wc Command

The wc command is usually used to display the total number of lines, the number of words, and total bytes in the files.

[mak567@localhost ~]$ wc ls-otpt.txt

The command mentioned above will display three numbers, such as lines, words, and bytes that the ls-otpt.txt contains. It the wc command is executed without command-line arguments, it accepts standard input. The –l option in the command limits the output to report just the lines.

The grep Command

The grep command is used to find text patterns that are within the text patterns files. When grep encounters a particular pattern in the file, it tends to print out the lines that contain it. The pattern that the grep command can catch vary from simple to complex. You can use the grep command in the following manner.

[mak567@localhost ~]$ ls /beef /usr/beef | sort | uniq | grep zip

Miscellaneous Commands

Sometimes, you don't need the full output of a command to be displayed on the screen of the shell. In this case, you can use a special command to see just the first bunch of lines and the last bunch of lines of the output of the command. If you want to see the first bunch of lines, you can use the head command. If you want to see the last bunch of lines, you can use the tail command. As a rule, both commands display at least ten lines on the shell screen. However, you can adjust the number of lines by using the –n option. Let's see how to write the command in the shell.

[mak567@localhost ~]$ head –n 15 ls-otpt.txt

In the above command, I attempted to display the first 15 lines of the output of the file ls-otpt.txt. Here is the sample command to display the last ten lines of the same file.

[mak567@localhost ~]$ tail –n 15 ls-otpt.txt

The tail command helps view how log files have been doing as they are written.

You can check out the documentation of each command that you have gone through in the chapter. I just talked about the basic usage of each command, but they have a great number of interesting options that you can explore by reading the documentation. It is generally said that Linux is all about flexing the muscle of your imagination. While the Windows operating system is stubborn and static, the Linux operation system offers you flexibility. Windows is like a store, from which you can buy ready-made things that are shiny, useful but are unchangeable. After a while, you start getting tired of a lack of change. You get bored and discard it and buy a new version of it when it is available. The practice goes on endlessly. You often complain to the store owner that the system just cannot be changed, and each time you get the same reply that the creator won't let you change it.

On the other hand, Linux gives you all the flexibility of the world. You can open it and enjoy a huge collection of different parts that you can play with, construct things, and create new programs. It is like a set of tools that you can use to create custom things that make you feel happy. After a while, you find out the right ideas to make the right things. For people who love graphics more than a dark screen, it can be boring.

Chapter Five

Delving Deeper Into
the World of Shell

This chapter will walk you through the depths of the Linux shell. Each time you type something in the command line and press the ENTER key, the bash performs multiple processes upon the text before you carry out the command. The process, which does all that is known as expansion. With the help of expansion, you can enter something in the shell, and the shell then expands that something into a bigger thing even before the shell acts on it. For example, as already discussed, the echo command is a built-in for Linux shell. It performs really simple tasks such as it prints text arguments. This is a very straightforward task. You enter a piece of text, and the echo command will echo the same by repeating it on the shell screen. If you add * to the echo command, things will be different. The * is a wildcard character, which means that the shell should match any characters in a file name. The shell expands the * command into the names of files that exist inside of the current working directory. It does that before the execution of the command. When you press the ENTER key, the shell will expand the qualifying characters on your command line before you carry out the command.

The mechanism is known as pathname expansion. The filenames that begin with a period of character are generally hidden. Pathname expansion tends to respect this special kind of behavior.

The Tilde Expansion

The tilde expansion of the cd command is something that has a special meaning in Linux shell. When it is used at the start of some random word, it generally expands into the name of a home directory of a user or the home directory of the current user.

[mak567@localhost ~]$ echo ~

Arithmetic

Linux shell allows you to perform certain arithmetic operations. It allows you arithmetic that is generally performed with the help of expansion. It allows you to use the shell prompt just like a calculator. In the following example, I will perform multiple arithmetic functions in the shell to see how the calculator works. The general expression is as under:

$((expression))

That's how you have to write it in the shell to execute it.

[mak567@localhost ~]$ echo $((2 + 2))

4

[mak567@localhost ~]$ echo $((2 * 2))

4

[mak567@localhost ~]$ echo $((2 - 2))

0

[mak567@localhost ~]$ echo $((2 ** 2))

4

[mak567@localhost ~]$ echo $((2 % 2))

0

[mak567@localhost ~]$ echo $((2 / 2))

1

[mak567@localhost ~]$ echo $(($((2 / 2)) + 55))

56

[mak567@localhost ~]$ echo $(($((2 + 2)) * 55))

220

[mak567@localhost ~]$ echo $(($((2 * 2)) + 55))

59

[mak567@localhost ~]$ echo $(($((2 - 2)) / 55))

0

[mak567@localhost ~]$ echo $(($((2 ** 2)) ** 55))

0

Now see another version of the same with some added text to it.

[mak567@localhost ~]$ echo Two plus two is equal two $((
2 + 2))

Two plus two is equal two 4

[mak567@localhost ~]$ echo Two multiply by Two is equal to $((2 * 2))

Two multiply by Two is equal to 4

[mak567@localhost ~]$ echo Two minus two is equal to $((2 - 2))

Two minus two is equal to 0

[mak567@localhost ~]$ echo the percentage of 2 over 2 is equal to $((2 % 2))

the percentage of 2 over 2 is equal to 0

[mak567@localhost ~]$ echo $(($((2 + 2)) * 55))

220

[mak567@localhost ~]$ echo divide two by two and then add it to fifty-five $(($((2 / 2)) + 55))

divide two by two and then add it to fifty-five 56

[mak567@localhost ~]$ echo multiply two with two and then add it to fifty-five
$(($((2 * 2)) + 55))

multiply two with two and then add it to fifty-five 59

```
[mak567@localhost ~]$ echo minus two by two and then ad
d it to fifty-five $(($(((

2 - 2 )) / 55))
```

minus two by two and then add it to fifty-five 0

Parameter Expansion

Parameter expansion is the most used expansion in shell scripting rather than on the command line. It allows the system to store small chunks of data and then give each chunk a particular name. Many chunks, also named as variables, are available for the examination. The variable, namely USER, tends to contain the username. To invoke the parameter expansion, you can use the command like the following.

```
[mak567@localhost ~]$ echo $USER
```

Double Quotes

The first type of quoting that you need to look into is double-quotes. If you need to place the text inside of the double quotes, you need all special characters that are being used by the shell, lose their special meaning. They should be treated as ordinary characters. You can cope up with the names of files that contain embedded spaces. For example, a file that is named *four horses.txt* has embedded spaces. If you try to use it on the command line, the shell would treat it as two individual arguments. However, you can resolve the problem by adding double quotes to the same on the command line.

Double quotes will cease the splitting of words and get you the desired result. You also can change the name of the file and remove the embedded spaces to remove the hassle next time.

[mak567@localhost ~]$ ls –l "four horses.txt."

[mak567@localhost ~]$ mv "four horses.txt"
four_horses.txt

When you have done that, you don't have to use the same pesky double quotes in your future writing of commands. In any case, if you want to suppress all kinds of expansions, you should use single quotes.

Escaping Characters

Sometimes, you intend to quote a single character. To do this, you can precede the particular character with a backslash that is in context with the escape character. The backslash character is also used to represent control nodes. The first 32 characters that exist in the ASCII coding scheme are generally used for transmission of commands to teletype-like devices.

Keyboard Tricks in Linux

Linux is an operating system that keyboard lovers appreciate. The command line is no fun to you if you are not comfortable with plenty of typing each day. Command-line users love to use short commands that can help them get done certain things in the operating system. For example, you have read about different commands such as mv, ls, type, and rm.

You can do most of your work by using the fewest keystrokes. A major goal of Linux is never to have to lift your fingers from your keyboard. You will not need a mouse for normal operations. Here is a rundown of a bunch of common commands.

Editing

Let us take a look at some common keyboard commands that will help you get certain things done.

- ALT-F it will move the cursor forward by one word.

- ALT-B it will move the cursor backward by one word.

- CTRL-A it will move the cursor to the start of a line.

- CTRL-F it will move the cursor forward by one character.

- CTRL-E it will move the cursor to the end of a line.

- CTRL-L it will clear the screen.

- CTRL-D it will delete the character to the location of the cursor.

- CTRL-T it will transpose the character to the location of the cursor.

- ALT-U it will convert into uppercase the characters from the location of the cursor backward to the end.

- ALT-T it will transpose the word at the location of the cursor with one that had been preceding it.

- ALT-L it will convert into lowercase the characters from the location of the cursor to the end of a word on the command shell.

- CTRL-U it will kill text at the location of the cursor right to the start of the line.

- CTRL-K it will kill text at the location of the cursor right to the end of the line.

- ALT-D it will kill text at the location of the cursor right to the end of a word.

- ALT-BACKSPACE it will kill text at the location of the cursor right to the end of the word. If the cursor is at the start of a word instead of the middle, it will kill the previous word. So stay cautious while you use this command.

History

While you explore the world of Linux administration, you can view the contents of the list of history as well.

[mak567@localhost ~]$ history | less

The bash tends to store the past 500 commands that you have entered.

- CTRL-N it will move you to the next history entry, performing the same action as the down arrow.

- CTRL-P it will move you to the history entry, performing the same action as the up arrow.

- CTRL-R it will move you to the reverse incremental search, searching incrementally from the present command right up the list of history.

- ALT-< it will move to the top of the list of history.

- ALT-> it will move to the bottom of the list of history.

- ALT-Nit is used to conduct a forward search and non-incremental search.

- ALT-P it is used to conduct revers and non-incremental search. With the help of the key, you can type the search string and then press ENTER before you have performed the search.

Keyboard Shortcuts

There are a few simple keyboard shortcuts that can make your far easier and efficient in Linux. Lots of Linux users are experts in keyboard usage. Here is a rundown of a few keyboard shortcuts that you can use in Linux and improve your experience.

CTRL + ALT + BACKSPACE

You can use this shortcut trick when your Linux is not responding, or a program has got stuck or locked up on the desktop. Simply put, hit these keys if you just cannot get anything to respond to you. The combination will instantly log you out of X, and you will be redirected to the log in screen from where you can take a fresh start. Keep in mind that this shortcut is specific to window managers and desktop environments.

ALT + TAB

The shortcut allows you to run through all the open windows only to stop at the one on which you need to put your focus. In simple words, you cannot just grab the mouse and click to get a window focus. To cycle through your windows, you need to hold down the Alt key and afterward press the Tab key until you land on the window that you want to. This shortcut also works in window managers and desktop environments.

> [mak567@localhost ~]$ printenv | less

This shows the variables and their values. The set command, on the other hand, when used without any arguments or options, will generally display the shell as well as environment variables. It will also display any kind of defined shell variables. Unlike the printenv command, its output is sorted in alphabetical order. You also can view the contents of a solitary variable by using the echo command, just like the following.

> [mak567@localhost ~]$ echo $HOME

Chapter Six

Configuration and Environment

The shell generally maintains a body of information during the shell session dubbed as the environment. The data stored in a Linux environment is commonly used by a set of programs to determine different facts about configuration. Most programs tend to use configuration files to store the program settings. Some programs will look out for values that are stored in the environment to adjust the behavior.

The shell environment stores different types of data, known as environment variables as well as shell variables. Shell variables also store a bunch of programmatic data, namely aliases, as well as shell functions. You take a look at what you are in your particular Linux environment. Either you can use set or the printenv programs to view data that exist in the environment. The set command tends to show the shell as well as the environment variables. The printenv command tends to display the latter. The list of the environment variables is going to be a long one, which is why it the right thing to pipe the output.

Environment Variables

The environment generally contains a little number of variables, such as the following:

DISPLAY

It is the name of your display screen if you are operating a graphical environment.

SHELL

It is the name of the shell program in which you write commands and customize your Linux operating system.

LANG

The LANG variable defines the collation and character set of the language you are using in the system.

PAGER

It is the name of the program that needs to be used for paging output.

HOME

This variable is the pathname of the home directory that you have been using.

EDITOR

It is the name of some program that needs to be used for text editing.

OLD_PWD

It refers to the previous directory.

PATH

It is a colon-separated list of different directories that usually are searched when you or any other user enter the name of any executable program.

USER

It is your own username in the Linux system.

PS1

This variable will prompt String 1. It will also define the contents of the shell prompt. You can customize this one as per your needs.

TZ

This variable tends to specify your time zone.

TERM

It is the name of any terminal type. This variable has the capability of setting the protocols that are to be used with the terminal emulator.

Establishing Environment

When you log on to your Linux system, the bash program kicks off and starts reading different configuration scripts that are known as startup files. They define the default environment, which is shared by the users. This step is followed by a bunch of startup files in the home directory that usually define the personal environment. The exact sequence of the files depends on the shell session type.

The shell sessions are of two types: login session and non-login session. A login shell session is the one in which you are prompted for the username and the password. When you start a virtual console session, you have to enter your usernames and passwords. A non-login session is the one that typically occurs when you launch a terminal session in the GUI. A login session reads one of the more of the startup files. Similarly, a non-login session has its own set of files to read from. In addition to reading the startup files, a non-login session inherits a Linux environment from the parent process. You need to take a look at the system and see which startup files you possess. You will be needing to use the -a option when you are using ls.

As Linux allows you to see what do the startup files contain and how the files look, you can modify them. You can add directories to your path and also define some additional variables. You can place all the changes in the .bash_profile.

Editors

The text editors are for you to edit the startup files of the shell. You also can edit some configuration files on your system. A text editor is generally a program that allows you to edit the words on your screen with the help of a moving cursor. It tends to differ from a word processor as it supports only pure text, and more often, it contains different features such that it is designed for writing different computer programs. Text editors are the main tools that software developers use for writing code. System administrators also use it to manage a set of configuration files that tend to control the system. There are a lot of text editors available in the market that you can purchase and install on Linux. Since the text editors in Linux are generally used by programmers, the developers of the editors have been introducing significant changes to the editors to suit the needs of programmers.

Text editors fall into a couple of basic categories; the first one is graphical, which is based on text. KDE and GNOME come under the umbrella of graphical editors. GNOME comes with the editor gedit, which is a text editor. KDE has three editors which have different levels of complexity. These editors are named as kwrite, kedit, and kate.

There is no shortage of text-based editors. The highly popular ones of them are emacs, nano, and vi. The nano editor is very simple and easy-to-use. The vi editor that is found on a majority of the Linux systems is the traditional editor for the Linux system. The emacs editor was written originally by Richard Stallman. It is a giant-sized editor that also is does-everything type stuff. It is readily available, but it is not something that comes installed on Linux by default.

You can invoke a text editor by writing a command in the command line. Just type the name of the editor, followed by the name of the file that you are looking forward to editing. If the said file doesn't exist, the editor will most likely assume that you are looking forward to creating a new file.

[mak567@localhost ~]$ vi random-file

The command will open the vi editor and load the file that I have mentioned. You can do the same if you have a file waiting to be opened up. Almost all graphical text editors generally are self-explanatory. You can explore and get to know them quite easily.

If you want to learn about Linux administration, you cannot pick up all the tips and tricks while taking a stroll in the afternoon and reading a book. It takes basic knowledge of the topics and great practice. In the next chapter, I will introduce you to 'vi.' One of the top core programs that you come across in Linux is the 'vi' text editor.

Why vi?

The first version of vi rolled out in 1976. It was Bill Joy, a student from the University of California Berkeley, who would, later on, co-found the Sun Microsystems. The text editor has got its name from the English word 'visual.' Initially, it was intended to allow editing on video terminals.

This is the age of graphical editors and some easy-to-use interface like nano, then why do you need vi? There are plenty of nice reasons for it. The vi text editor is always available. This tends to be a lifesaver if you have a system that has no graphical interface like a remote server or a local system that has a broken X configuration. The nano text editor is popular, but it is not yet universal.

Vi is fast and lightweight. You can use it for many tasks as it is easier to bring up vi than it is to locate the graphical text editor in menus and then wait for multiple megabytes before it loads. This text editor is specifically designed for the typing speed as well.

Most Linux administrations don't include vi. Rather they go on to ship its enhanced version named vim. The vim is a substantial improvement as compared to vi. You can start it by a simple command in the command line.

[mak567@localhost ~]$ vi

To save the current text to a file, you can enter the 'insert mode.' Press the I key on the keyboard then see if the editor is running at the bottom of your screen. When the editor is in command mode, it offers different movements of commands. Here is a rundown of some of them.

- J denotes the down arrow, and you can use it to move down by one line on the editor.

- K denotes the up arrow, and you can use it to move up by one line on the editor.

- H denotes the left side arrow, and it tends to move one character to the right side.

- L denotes the right side arrow, and it tends to move one character to the left side.

- W takes you to the start of the next word or a punctuation character.

- 0 (zero) lands you at the start of the current line.

- If you press SHIFT-6(^), you will move the cursor to the first non-whitespace character found on the current line.

- If you press SHIFT-W(w), you will move the cursor to the start of the next word while ignoring the punctuation characters.

- If you press SHIFT-4($), you will move the cursor to the end of the present line.

- B is for moving the cursor to the start of the last word or the punctuation mark.

- If you press SHIFT-B(B), you will move the cursor to the start of the past word but will ignore any punctuation mark along the way.

- If you press CTRL-B or PAGE UP, you will move the cursor one page on the upside.

- If you press CTRL-F or PAGE DOWN, you will move the cursor one page on the downside.

- If you press SHIFT-G(G), you will move the cursor to the last line of the content of the file you are currently working in.

- If you press number-SHIFT-G, you will move the cursor to a specific line number. For example, 2G will take you to the second line of the file. 1G will take you to the first line while 4G will take you to the fourth line of the file.

Basic Editing

There are several ways by which you can enter the insert mode and start editing text. The basic mode is to use the 'I' command to enter the insert mode. Suppose there is goof.txt named file stored on your computer. If you want to add text to the end of a sentence, the i command is not going to help you in that case because it will not move the cursor beyond a certain line. The vi editor offers a specific command to enter insert mode. If you move the cursor to the end of the line and type a, vi will enter the insert mode. Now you can add the extra text if you want to. Any time if you want to exit the insert mode, you can press the ESC button to shoot off the insert mode. When you are editing the text, you almost always require to append text to the end of a line. That's why vi offers you a shortcut to move to the end of the line and start the appending process. You can enter A to kick off the appending process. You can add as many lines as you require. In the first move, you will move the cursor to the start of the line by using the zero command. Then type A and add more lines. When you are done with that, press ESC to exit this mode. The A command is more useful because it tends to move to the end of the line before the insert mode starts.

You can open a new line and insert text there, by using the o and O commands. The o command will open a line under the current line while the O command will open a line right above the current line. That's how it allows you to add as much text as you want to.

When you use a text editor, it is highly likely that you have to delete some text at some point. The vi editor offers several ways to delete a piece of text. The first method is to use the X key, which will delete a character where the cursor at the moment resides. You can add a number before x to specify how many characters ought to be deleted. There is a D key that denotes a more general purpose. Just like x, it ought to be preceded by a number that would specify the total number of times the deletion ought to be performed. You also can use 'd' plus a movement command that controls the size of your deletion. Here is a rundown of some commands to perform deletion in the editor.

- Command x deletes the current character.

- The command 3x deletes the current character along with the following two characters.

- The command dd deletes the entire line at which you currently keep the cursor.

- The command 5dd deletes the entire line at which you currently keep the cursor and also the next four lines in the editor.

- The command d$ deletes the text from the present location of the cursor to the end of the current line.

- The command d^ deletes the text from the present location of the cursor to the first non-whitespace character in the current line.

- The command dG deletes the text from the current line to the end of the current file.

- The command d0 deletes the text from the present location of the cursor to the start of the current line.

- The command dW deletes the text from the present location of the cursor to the start of the next word in the line.

- The command d20G deletes the text from the current line to the 20th line of a file.

You can use the d command to cut the text from one spot and to paste it at another location. The deletion is generally copied in a paste buffer from which you can paste it at another point by entering the p command after the cursor. Use the P command to paste it before the cursor.

Linux offers a variety of yanking (copying) commands to its users. Here is a rundown of all these commands that you can use while you are editing in Linux.

- If you enter yy on the Linux command line, you will be able to copy the current line.

- If you enter 5yy on the Linux command line, you will be able to copy the current line along with the next four lines. This makes five lines as indicated by the digit 5.

- If you enter y$ on the Linux command line, you will be able to copy the text from the point your cursor stands now to the point where the current line ends.

- If you enter y^ on the Linux command line, you will be able to copy the text from the point your cursor stands now to the point where the first non-whitespace character is found.

- If you enter yG on the Linux command line, you will be able to copy the text from the point your cursor stands now to the point where the file ends.

- If you enter y0 on the Linux command line, you will be able to copy the text from the point your cursor stands now to the starting point of the file.

- If you enter yW on the Linux command line, you will be able to copy the text from the point your cursor stands now to the next word in the file.

- If you enter y20G on the Linux command line, you will be able to copy the text from the point your cursor stands now to the 20th line of the file.

While making changes in the text editor, you always can enter the u command to undo any change. You can move the cursor in vi to locations on the base of your searches. You can either do this on a single line or an entire file. You also can perform text replacements with or without proper confirmation from the user. Use the f command to search a line and move the cursor to the next instance of a character that you specify. The command fa would move the cursor to the next occurrence of the character 'a.' After you have performed a character inside a line, you can repeat the search just by entering a semicolon.

You can use an ex command in vi to perform search-and-replace operations that are also called substitution in vi. If you want to change a word for the entire file, you can enter Line to line command.

:%s/Line/line/g is the command that allows you to make changes throughout the entire file.

The colon : character in the command kicks off an ex command. The % character in the command specifies the range of lines in the operation. The % command is generally a shortcut, which means you want to introduce the change from the first to the last line. Alternatively, you can specify the change like 1, 5, or like 1, $, which means that you need to introduce the change from the first to the last line of the file. The s character in the command specifies your operation. In this case, the specification is of the search and replace operation. The /Line/line/ denotes the search pattern and also the replacement text. The g character means global. It means you want to perform the substitution process to each instance of the search string throughout the file.

Customization of Prompt

You will be able to learn how you can customize the shell prompt. A thorough examination reveals the inner workings of the Linux shell and the terminal emulator program. Just like so many other things in the Linux operating system, the shell prompt tends to be highly configurable. The prompt is a really useful device if you learn to control it. The default prompt looks something like the following.

[mak567@localhost ~]$

There are a username, hostname, and the current working directory.

Escape Codes

- The sequence \h will display the name of the host of the local machine minus the domain name.

- The sequence \a will display the ASCII bell, which makes your computer beep when it feels encountered.

- The sequence \H will display the full name of the host of the local machine.

- The sequence \j will display the total number of jobs that the current shell session is currently running and managing.

- The sequence \d will display the current date, the day, the month in a proper format.

- The sequence \u will display the username of the current user of the machine.

- The sequence \A will display the current time in hours and minutes format. It will display the time in the 24-hour format.

- The sequence \@ will display the current time in AM/PM 12 hour format.

- The sequence \T will display the current time in a simple 12 hours format.

- The sequence \t will display the current time in 24-hour format with clearly displaying the hours, minutes, and seconds as well.

- The sequence \l will display the name of your current terminal device.

- The sequence \n will display a newline character.

- The sequence \s will display the name of the shell program.

- The sequence \r will display a carriage return.

- The sequence \w will display the name of your present working directory.

- The sequence \v will display the version number of Linux shell.

- The sequence \V will display the version as well as the release numbers of Linux shell.

- The sequence \] will display the signals of the end of any non-printing sequence of characters.

- The sequence \[will signal the beginning of a series of single or multiple non-printing characters. It is used to embed some non-printing control characters that could manipulate a terminal emulator in one or the other way, like moving your cursor or changing the colors of the text.

- The sequence \W will display the last part of the name of the current working directory.

- The sequence \# will display the total number of commands that you have entered during a single shell session.

- The sequence \$ will display a $ character unless you enjoy superuser privileges.

Adding Colors

Many terminal emulator programs tend to respond to several non-printing character sequences to control character attributes like color and bold text and cursor position. The color of the character is usually controlled by sending an escape code embedded in the stream of characters that ought to be displayed. The control code is interpreted by the terminal emulator in the form of instruction. Let's take a look at the available text colors. Please note that the colors fall into two groups that are differentiated by boldness and lightness. Here is a rundown of how you can change the color by trying out different consequences.

- The sequence \033[0;30m will turn the text into black color.

- The sequence \033[0;31m will turn the text into red color.

- The sequence \033[0;32m will turn the text into green color.

- The sequence \033[0;33m will turn the text into brown color.

- The sequence \033[0;34m will turn the text into blue color.

- The sequence \033[0;35m will turn the text into purple color.

- The sequence \033[0;36m will turn the text into cyan color.

- The sequence \033[0;37m will turn the text into light gray color.

- The sequence \033[1;30m will turn the text into dark gray color.

- The sequence \033[1;31m will turn the text into light red color.

- The sequence \033[1;32m will turn the text into light green color.

- The sequence \033[1;33m will turn the text into yellow color.

- The sequence \033[1;34m will turn the text into light blue color.

- The sequence \033[1;35m will turn the text into light purple color.

- The sequence \033[1;36m will turn the text into light cyan color.

- The sequence \033[1;37m will turn the text into white color.

You also can change the background color by using the following sequence codes.

- The sequence \033[0;40m will turn the background into black color.

- The sequence \033[0;41m will turn the background into red color.

- The sequence \033[0;42m will turn the background into green color.

- The sequence \033[0;43m will turn the background into brown color.

- The sequence \033[0;44m will turn the background into blue color.

- The sequence \033[0;45m will turn the background into purple color.

- The sequence \033[0;46m will turn the background into cyan color.

- The sequence \033[0;47m will turn the background into light gray color.

Moving Cursor

You can move your cursor in Linux shell by using certain escape codes. This is the most common element in the Linux shell. Some common cursor movement escape sequences are as under:

- The escape sequence \033[1;cH will move the cursor on the screen to line 1 and column c.

- The escape sequence \033[nA will move the cursor on the screen up the n lines.

- The escape sequence \033[nB will move the cursor on the screen down the n lines.

- The escape sequence \033[nC will move the cursor to the forward side by n characters.

- The escape sequence \033[nD will move the cursor to the backside by n characters.

- The escape sequence \033[2J will clear up your shell screen and also move the cursor on the screen to the top-left corner that is at line 0 and column 0.

- The escape sequence \033[K will clear from the position of the cursor to the end of the present line.

- The escape sequence \033[s will store the present position of the cursor.

- The escape sequence \033[u will recall the position of the cursor at which you had stored it.

With the help of the codes mentioned above, you will be able to construct a prompt that would help you speed up your operations in Linux.

Chapter Seven

Writing Shell Scripts

The real challenge of the Linux administrative system lies in writing shell scripts by yourself. A shell script is generally a file that contains several commands. The shell reads through the file and carries out these commands as though they have entered them directly on their command line. The shell is a powerful command-line interface to the system as well as a scripting language interpreter. Most of the things that you can do on your command line can also be done in scripts.

You can write your shell scripts and run the same on the command line by following three steps. The first step is writing the script. Shell scripts generally are text files, so you need a text editor to write them. The best text editor offers syntax highlighting that would allow you to see a colored viewed of all the elements of the script. If you are a programmer and you know about Python, it would be easier for you to understand why highlighted text is important during writing a script. If you are new to programming or shell scripting, you will know the importance of different text color when you start writing your first script. It just facilitates reading and writing the code. Syntax highlighting also helps in spotting different kinds of errors.

The vim, gedit, and kate are some efficient contenders for writing shell scripts. The second step is to execute the scripts in the shell by setting the permission of the script file to allow the execution. The final step is to put the script at a place where the shell can easily find it. The shell searches several directories for executable files when there is no explicit pathname specification.

If you are practicing at the moment, you can fire up any online bash editor to create your scripts. Later on, you can download the one you like. Let us create the first shell script.

#!/bin/bash

This is my first script for Linux.

echo 'I am learning Linux shell scripting.'

Here is the result:

$bash -f main.sh

I am learning Linux shell scripting.

The last line of the script may appear to be familiar to you as it is the same echo command that you have learned at the start of the book. The echo command is generally a string argument with the second line being a comment. The next step is to make the script executable. This can be done by using the chmod command. Let us see how to do that.

[mak567@localhost ~]$ chmod 755 ls-otpt

Take a look at the permissions of shell scripts. 755 is for the scripts that everyone can execute while 700 is for the scripts that only the owner has the power to execute.

Formatting

One of the most important things that you must consider before moving on to serious scriptwriting is that you need to keep it neat and clean so that you can easily read when you come back next time. It facilitates easy maintenance.

The key to writing and using shell scripts is the ability to enter more than one command and yet be able to process the results for each command. You can chain together different commands. The shell shows how you can do that in a single step. If you want to enter two commands, you can enter then by using a semicolon. Make sure you add whitespace at the start and end of the semicolon to make it look neat and clean.

[mak567@localhost ~]$ date ; who

Thu May 7 08:02:01 UTC 2020

There are two bash shell commands in the script. The date command comes first, so it runs first and displays the date right away. You get to know the current date and time. Then comes the turn of the *who* command, which tells who is logged on in the system. By using this technique, you can tie together as many commands as you want to, and write a script. The maximum count of a single script is 255 characters. Although the technique is the best fit for a smaller script, it also has a drawback in that you will have to enter the full command at the prompt every time you have to run the script. Therefore, as a scriptwriter, you can create a text file and cram all the relevant commands in the file to avoid delays when you are using Linux in real-time for professional work. Whenever you need it, you just have to open and run the text file that carries the script.

Script File

To place all commands into a script file, you need a text editor. Create a file in the editor and then enter the commands in the same. When you are creating a file, you must specify the shell in which you have to use it. The basic format to specify the shell is as under:

#!/bin/bash

In the normal shell script line, you can use the pound sign as a comment line. The shell doesn't process the comment line. However, the first line of any shell script file is taken as a special case. The pound sign is usually followed by an exclamation mark that tells the shell what to do.

Long Name

Many of the commands that you have studied up till now have both short and long option names. The command ls has many options that can be expressed in the long and short forms. For example,

[mak567@localhost ~]$ ls -ad

You also can write the following command:

[mak567@localhost ~]$ ls –all --directory

These commands are equivalent. It means they bring the same results. The primary objective of using short command names over long command names is to cut down on the typing time. Short options are generally preferred upon when you enter options on your command line, but while writing scripts, you have to use the longer versions of commands to improve readability.

When you are using long commands, you can improve the readability of the text by spreading the text over multiple lines in the shell. You can apply this technique on the command line as well, although it is seldom used there. The major difference between the command line and a script is that a script employs tab characters for indentation purposes, whereas there is no place for tabs to activate completion.

You can configure vim for scriptwriting using the many configuration settings in the vim text editor. Several common options help you facilitate script writing. For example, you can use *:syntax on* to turn on the highlighting feature of syntax. With the help of this setting, you can display different elements of the shell syntax in a wide range of colors when you are viewing a particular script. This is quite helpful in identifying multiple kinds of programming errors. To make this feature work, you need to have a full version of vim installed on your system. The file you are working in needs to have a shebang, which indicates that the file happens to be a shell script.

- The :set hlsearch option turns on the option to highlight the search results. For example, you have searched the word 'echo.' If you have turned on this particular option, each instance of this word will be highlighted, and you can scan the entire file to find them easily.

- The :set autoindent option allows you to indent the entire file easily. This option allows vim to indent each new line in the same way the line has typed. This also speeds up typing on different kinds of programming constructs. If, at any point, you want to stop indentation, you can enter CTRL-D.

- The :set tabstop-4 command arranges the total number of columns that are occupied by a particular tab character. The default option is eight columns. You can set the value to 4, which allows long lines to fit easily on the screen of the editor.

All these changes can be made permanent by adding the commands to the ~/.vimrc file.

In this chapter, you learned how to write scripts in the text editor, how to format the same, and how to execute them on the system easily. You also saw how you could use different styles of formatting techniques to improve the readability of the scripts.

Chapter Eight

Structured Commands

You can see that the shell processes each command in the shell script in the order you write them. This is how you can be the master of sequential operations, where you need all of your commands to process them in the right order. Lots of programs demand some kind of logic flow control between different commands inside of the script. This means that the shell executes other commands in a set type of circumstances. Structured commands allow you to change the flow of operation of a program. It executes some commands under the right conditions while it skips other operations under certain conditions.

The if-then Statement

If you are familiar with Python or C language, you might have heard about the if-then statements. The format of the if-then statement in Linux different from other programming languages. The bash if statement tends to run the command that is defined on the if line. If the exit status of the command is zero, the commands listed are then executed. If the exit status is something else, then commands are usually not executed. Therefore the bash shell moves to the next command.

    cat

```
#!/bin/bash

# this is to test the if statement

if date

then

    echo "the command is functional"

fi

$bash -f main.sh
```

Thu May 7 03:58:55 UTC 2020

the command is functional

The script used the date command on the if line. If the command tends to complete successfully, the echo statement needs to display the text string. When you run the script on the command line, you will get the desired result. The shell will execute the date command, which he finds in the if line. Then it will execute the echo statement, which is listed in the then section. Let's check how the if-then statement works in Linux.

Note: In the next codes, I will display the result of each command right under the codes by partitioning it with (========)for you to easily understand that.

```
#This is to Initialize the two variables

x=50

y=70
```

#This is to check whether both are equal or not

if [$x == $y]

then

   echo "x has equal value to y"

fi

#This is to check whether both are not equal

if [$x != $y]

then

   echo "x has not the same value as b"

fi

$bash -f main.sh

x has not the same value as b

In the next code snippet, I will change the values of the variables to see which result I will get in the bash shell.

#This is to Initialize the two variables

x=50

y=50

#This is to check whether both are equal or not

```
if [ $x == $y ]

then

    echo "x has equal value to y"

fi


#This is to check whether both are not equal

if [ $x != $y ]

then

    echo "x has not the same value as b"

fi

$bash -f main.sh

x has equal value to y
```

Now I will move on to the next phase of conditionals that are introducing the if.else statement in the program. Let's see how you can write it and how you can make it work.

```
#This will Initialize two variables

x=30

y=30


if [ $x == $y ]

then
```

```
    #If the variables are equal in value, then you should print
this

    echo "x has equal value as that of y"
else

    echo "x does not have equal value as that of y"
fi
$bash -f main.sh
x has equal value as that of y
```

Now I will put unequal values for both variables.

```
    #This will Initialize two variables
x=25
y=30


if [ $x == $y ]
then

    #If the variables are equal in value, then you should print
this

    echo "x has equal value as that of y"
else

    echo "x does not have equal value as that of y"
fi
```

$bash -f main.sh

x does not have equal value as that of y

Example

```
#!/bin/bash

count=75

if [ $count -eq 50 ]

then

  echo "The total count is 75"

else

  echo "The total count is not 75"

fi

$bash -f main.sh

The total count is not 75
```

In the next example, I will give the variable the value of 75 to see how it reacts.

```
#!/bin/bash

count=75

if [ $count -eq 75 ]

then

  echo "The total count is 75"
```

else

  echo "The total count is not 75"

fi

$bash -f main.sh

The total count is 75

In the next example, I will explain the concepts of if-then, it-elif, and if-else statements in a single script file. Let's do some simple mathematics to see how the script works in the bash shell. I will be using two commands in the script. The command –eq denotes the equal sign while the command –gt denotes the greater sign, which will be a new addition to this script. Let us see how it works.

```
#!/bin/bash
count=600
if [ $count -eq 550 ]
then
  echo "The Count stands equal to 550"
elif [ $count -gt 550 ]
then
  echo "The Count stands greater than 550"
else
  echo "The Count stands less than 550"
fi
```

```
$bash -f main.sh
```

The Count stands greater than 550

Here is the next example with changed values.

```
#!/bin/bash

count=450

if [ $count -eq 550 ]

then

  echo "The Count stands equal to 550"

elif [ $count -gt 550 ]

then

  echo "The Count stands greater than 550"

else

  echo "The Count stands less than 550"

fi

$bash -f main.sh
```

The Count stands less than 550

In the next example, I will try another value for the script to see a different result.

```
#!/bin/bash

count=550

if [ $count -eq 550 ]
```

then

  echo "The Count stands equal to 550"

elif [$count -gt 550]

then

  echo "The Count stands greater than 550"

else

  echo "The Count stands less than 550"

fi

$bash -f main.sh

The Count stands equal to 550

Practical Applications of Conditionals

Bash conditional statements tend to perform many actions that depend on if a programmer-specified Boolean condition will true or false. With the help of bash conditionals, you can check if a certain file exists or not. You also can build a calculator by using if-else conditional statements in Python. You will have to fill in the program with the right input. Let's see how to build this program.

Double Parenthesis

The double parenthesis commands permit you to add advanced mathematical formulas in the comparisons.

cat #!/bin/bash

This is the way of using double parenthesis

```
valt=20
if (( $valt ** 2 > 90 ))
then
(( valx = $valt ** 2 ))
echo "The possible square of $valt is $valx"
fi
$bash -f main.sh
The possible square of 20 is 400
```

The for Command

The 'for' command in Linux helps you iterate through a series of commands. It happens that you may need to put a set of commands on repetition until a particular condition has been met, like processing of different files in a single directory and all users and all lines in a text file. The bash shell offers the for command that allows you to form a loop that would iterate through many values. Each iteration in the script will perform a defined set of commands by using one of its values. Let take a look at the format of the command.

```
for var in thelist
do
commands
done
```

In each iteration, the var variable tends to contain the present value in a list. The first iteration takes the first item from the list and uses it, the second iteration takes the second item, and it goes so on. That's how all the items on the list are iterated. The commands that you will use in between the do and the done statements can either be one or more of the standard bash $var commands. You may include a do and for statement on the same line, but you ought to separate it from the list items by using a semicolon. The simplest use of the for command is to iterate it through a bunch of values defined inside the for command. Let's take a look at an example.

```
cat testA

#!/bin/bash

# basic for command

for test in Texas Ohio Alabama New Jersey Alaska Arkansas Colorado California do

        echo Your next stop is at the American state of $test

        done

$ ./testA

Your next stop is at the American state of Texas

Your next stop is at the American state of Ohio

Your next stop is at the American state of Alabama

Your next stop is at the American state of New Jersey

Your next stop is at the American state of Alaska
```

Your next stop is at the American state of Arkansas

Your next stop is at the American state of Colorado

Your next stop is at the American state of California

$

Each time the for command makes an iteration through the list of values that are provided, it assigns the test variable to the next value that exists in the list. The test$ variable can also be used like other script variables inside of the for command statements.

```
cat
#!/bin/bash
# basic for command
for test in Texas Ohio Alabama New Jersey Alaska Arkansas Colorado California do
        echo Your next stop is at the American state of $test
        done
echo "The last state of your stop was $test"
test=Maine
echo "Now you are going to stop at $test"
$ ./test1
Your next stop is at the American state of Texas
Your next stop is at the American state of Ohio
```

Your next stop is at the American state of Alabama

Your next stop is at the American state of New Jersey

Your next stop is at the American state of Alaska

Your next stop is at the American state of Arkansas

Your next stop is at the American state of Colorado

Your next stop is at the American state of California

The last state of your stop was California

Now you are going to stop at Maine

$

You can read some complex values from the inside of a list. In the next example, I will form a list of all the states that you have to stop at in Linux. After I have accumulated it, I will run the iteration through the list. I will take the past example and introduce the necessary changes in it. You should keep in mind that the name that follows cat in the first line of code is the name of the file that you can change as per your will. I have created this file in a Linux text editor. You can do the same. Let's see how to do that.

```
cat
#!/bin/bash
# I will now use a variable for holding the list.
list ="Texas Ohio Alabama New Jersey Alaska Arkansas Colorado California"
```

```
list=$list" Maine"

for test in

do

echo "Your next stop is at the American state of $test"

done
```

================

```
$ ./test1

Your next stop is at the American state of Texas

Your next stop is at the American state of Ohio

Your next stop is at the American state of Alabama

Your next stop is at the American state of New Jersey

Your next stop is at the American state of Alaska

Your next stop is at the American state of Arkansas

Your next stop is at the American state of Colorado

Your next stop is at the American state of California

Your next stop is at the American state of Maine

$
```

Read Values Right From a Command

There is another way by which you can generate values for your personal use. In this method, you have to use the output of a particular command. You can use certain backtick characters to execute a command that can produce a certain output. Then you can use the same output of a command in the for loop. Let's see how to do that.

```
cat

#!/bin/bash

# This script will read certain values from a particular file.

myfile="states"

for state in `cat $myfile`

do

echo "Your next stop is at the American state of $myfile"

done

        cat states

Texas

Ohio

Alabama

New Jersey

Alaska

Arkansas

Colorado

California

$ ./test1
```

Your next stop is at the American state of Texas

Your next stop is at the American state of Ohio

Your next stop is at the American state of Alabama

Your next stop is at the American state of New Jersey

Your next stop is at the American state of Alaska

Your next stop is at the American state of Arkansas

Your next stop is at the American state of Colorado

Your next stop is at the American state of California

$

In this example, I have used the cat command for displaying the contents of myfile. The for command iterates through the output of cat command, doing that by one line at a time.

Field Separator

The reason behind this problem is a special environment variable IFS also known as the internal field separator. This variable defines particular lit of characters that the bash shell uses as field separators. The bash shell considers the following characters as field separators; a space, a newline, and a new tab. To solve this particular problem, you can change the values of the IFS environment variable in the shell script for restriction of the characters that the bash shell identifies as field separators. If you want a change in the IFS value to recognize the newline character, you ought to do this.

IFS=$'\n'

Now let's apply the same at the example that we have been using for quite some time.

```
cat test1
#!/bin/bash
# This script will read certain values from a particular file.
myfile="states"
IFS=$'\n'
for state in 'cat $myfile'
echo "Your next stop is at the American state of $myfile"
done
$ ./test1
Your next stop is at the American state of Texas
Your next stop is at the American state of Ohio
Your next stop is at the American state of Alabama
Your next stop is at the American state of New Jersey
Your next stop is at the American state of Alaska
Your next stop is at the American state of Arkansas
Your next stop is at the American state of Colorado
Your next stop is at the American state of California
$
```

The while Command

The while command is like a cross between the for loop and the if-then statement. The while command generally allows you first to define a command and then loop through a set of commands for as long as the commands return a zero status. The while command tests each iteration, and when it arrives at the non-zero return status, it will stop further execution of the commands. The basic while command format is as under:

while test command

do

many other commands

done

The format may look like an if-then statement from the conditionals section. You can use any bash shell command for this one. The key is that the exit status must change based on the commands that are running the loop. If the exit status doesn't change, the while loop command will turn into an infinite loop. You won't want to get stuck in an infinite loop, for sure. Let's see how to create a script by using the while command.

cat #!/bin/bash

I am testing the while command

vart=25

while [$vart -gt 0]

```
do

echo $vart

vart=$[ $vart - 1 ]

done

$bash -f main.sh

25

24

23

22

21

20

19

18

17

16

15

14

13

12

11

10
```

9

8

7

6

5

4

3

2

1

You can change the variable difference from -1 to -2 and see the changing the results. Let us see how to do that.

```
cat #!/bin/bash
# I am testing the while command
vart=25
while [ $vart -gt 0 ]
do
echo $vart
vart=$[ $vart - 2 ]
done
```

$bash -f main.sh

25

23

21

19

17

15

13

11

9

7

5

3

1

Example

```
#!/bin/bash
```

while-menu: this is a menu-driven system information program

DELAY=3 # This is the Number of seconds needed to display the results

```
while [[ $REPLY != 0 ]]; do
```

```
clear

cat <<- _EOF_
```

Please Select:

1. This will display the System Information

2. This will display the Display Disk Space

3. This will display the Display Home Space Utilization

0. Quit

```
    _EOF_

read -p "Please Enter the selection [0-3] > "

if [[ $REPLY =~ ^[0-3]$ ]]; then

if [[ $REPLY == 1 ]]; then

echo "This is the Hostname: $HOSTNAME"

uptime

sleep $DELAY

fi

if [[ $REPLY == 2 ]]; then

df -h

sleep $DELAY

fi
```

```
if [[ $REPLY == 3 ]]; then

if [[ $(id -u) -eq 0 ]]; then

echo "This is the Home Space Utilization (All Users)"

du -sh /home/*

else

echo "This is the Home Space Utilization ($USER)"

du -sh $HOME

fi

sleep $DELAY

fi

else

echo "This displays the Invalid entry."

sleep $DELAY

fi

done

echo "This will show that the Program has been
terminated."
```

$bash -f main.sh

Please Select:

1. This will display the System Information

2. This will display the Display Disk Space

3. This will display the Display Home Space Utilization

0. Quit

This displays the Invalid entry.

Please Select:

1. This will display the System Information

2. This will display the Display Disk Space

3. This will display the Display Home Space Utilization

0. Quit

This displays the Invalid entry.

Please Select:

1. This will display the System Information

2. This will display the Display Disk Space

3. This will display the Display Home Space Utilization

0. Quit

This displays the Invalid entry.

Please Select:

1. This will display the System Information

2. This will display the Display Disk Space

3. This will display the Display Home Space Utilization

0. Quit

This displays the Invalid entry.

Multiple Commands

The while loop allows you to run multiple commands. Just the exit status of the final command is generally used for determination of when the while loop stops. This can trigger a blend of interesting results in case you don't take due care. Let's see an example.

```
cat #!/bin/bash

# Now I am going to test a multicommand while loop

vart=20

while echo $vart

[ $vart -ge 0 ]

do

echo "This number falls inside of a loop"

vart=$[ $vart - 1 ]

done

$bash -f main.sh
```

20

This number falls inside of a loop

19

This number falls inside of a loop

18

This number falls inside of a loop

17

This number falls inside of a loop

16

This number falls inside of a loop

15

This number falls inside of a loop

14

This number falls inside of a loop

13

This number falls inside of a loop

12

This number falls inside of a loop

11

This number falls inside of a loop

10

This number falls inside of a loop

9

This number falls inside of a loop

8

This number falls inside of a loop

7

This number falls inside of a loop

6

This number falls inside of a loop

5

This number falls inside of a loop

4

This number falls inside of a loop

3

This number falls inside of a loop

2

This number falls inside of a loop

1

This number falls inside of a loop

0

This number falls inside of a loop

-1

In the next example, I will use a change of -2 in the second loop. See how it works.

```
cat #!/bin/bash

# Now I am going to test a multicommand while loop

vart=20

while echo $vart

[ $vart -ge 0 ]

do

echo "This number falls inside of a loop"

vart=$[ $vart - 2 ]

done

$bash -f main.sh

20

This number falls inside of a loop

18

This number falls inside of a loop

16

This number falls inside of a loop

14

This number falls inside of a loop

12

This number falls inside of a loop

10
```

This number falls inside of a loop

8

This number falls inside of a loop

6

This number falls inside of a loop

4

This number falls inside of a loop

2

This number falls inside of a loop

0

This number falls inside of a loop

-2

I used two test commands in a while statement, the first displaying the current value of the vart variable. The second one uses the test command to determine the real value of the same variable. I inserted an echo statement inside the loop that indicated that the loop had been processed. The while loop executes the same statement for when the variable has zero value. The test commands generally were executed for the next iterations.

The until Command

The 'until' command works the opposite way than that of the while command. This one requires that you ought to specify a particular test command that would produce non-zero exit status. As long as the status is non-zero, the bash shell executes these commands within the loop. Once it reaches zero exit status, it ceases to work. You also can add one more test command in the until command statement. The exit status of the past command tends to determine if the bash shell can execute other defined commands or not.

```
cat #!/bin/bash

# Now I am going to use the until command

vart=50

until [ $vart -eq 0 ]

do

echo $vart

vart=$[ $vart - 2 ]

done
```

$bash -f main.sh

```
50

48

46

44

42

40
```

38

36

34

32

30

28

26

24

22

20

18

16

14

12

10

8

6

4

2

In the next example, I will use multiple tests with the until command. Let's see how it goes.

cat #!/bin/bash

Here is another example of the until command

vart=50

until echo $vart

[$vart -eq 0]

do

echo This is still inside of the loop: $vart

vart=$[$vart - 2]

done

$bash -f main.sh

50

This is still inside of the loop: 50

48

This is still inside of the loop: 48

46

This is still inside of the loop: 46

44

This is still inside of the loop: 44

42

This is still inside of the loop: 42

40

This is still inside of the loop: 40

38

This is still inside of the loop: 38

36

This is still inside of the loop: 36

34

This is still inside of the loop: 34

32

This is still inside of the loop: 32

30

This is still inside of the loop: 30

28

This is still inside of the loop: 28

26

This is still inside of the loop: 26

24

This is still inside of the loop: 24

22

This is still inside of the loop: 22

20

This is still inside of the loop: 20

18

This is still inside of the loop: 18

16

This is still inside of the loop: 16

14

This is still inside of the loop: 14

12

This is still inside of the loop: 12

10

This is still inside of the loop: 10

8

This is still inside of the loop: 8

6

This is still inside of the loop: 6

4

This is still inside of the loop: 4

2

This is still inside of the loop: 2

0

You can take it to the next level by increasing the upper threshold. Let's see how it reacts when I replace the figure 50 with 90. I will keep the rest of the script the same. Here are the script and its result in the shell.

```
vart=90

until echo $vart

[ $vart -eq 0 ]

do

echo This is still inside of the loop: $vart

vart=$[ $vart - 2 ]

done
```

$bash -f main.sh

```
90

This is still inside of the loop: 90

88

This is still inside of the loop: 88

86

This is still inside of the loop: 86

84

This is still inside of the loop: 84

82
```

This is still inside of the loop: 82

80

This is still inside of the loop: 80

78

This is still inside of the loop: 78

76

This is still inside of the loop: 76

74

This is still inside of the loop: 74

72

This is still inside of the loop: 72

70

This is still inside of the loop: 70

68

This is still inside of the loop: 68

66

This is still inside of the loop: 66

64

This is still inside of the loop: 64

62

This is still inside of the loop: 62

60

This is still inside of the loop: 60

58

This is still inside of the loop: 58

56

This is still inside of the loop: 56

54

This is still inside of the loop: 54

52

This is still inside of the loop: 52

50

This is still inside of the loop: 50

48

This is still inside of the loop: 48

46

This is still inside of the loop: 46

44

This is still inside of the loop: 44

42

This is still inside of the loop: 42

40

This is still inside of the loop: 40

38

This is still inside of the loop: 38

36

This is still inside of the loop: 36

34

This is still inside of the loop: 34

32

This is still inside of the loop: 32

30

This is still inside of the loop: 30

28

This is still inside of the loop: 28

26

This is still inside of the loop: 26

24

This is still inside of the loop: 24

22

This is still inside of the loop: 22

20

This is still inside of the loop: 20

18

This is still inside of the loop: 18

16

This is still inside of the loop: 16

14

This is still inside of the loop: 14

12

This is still inside of the loop: 12

10

This is still inside of the loop: 10

8

This is still inside of the loop: 8

6

This is still inside of the loop: 6

4

This is still inside of the loop: 4

2

This is still inside of the loop: 2

0

So virtually, there is no limit to the upper threshold of calculations in Linux.

Nesting Loops

A loop statement can make use of other commands by nesting them inside of them. The nested commands can be loops as well. You need to care extreme care while you are using nested loops because you have to perform an iteration inside of an integration. So that's two iterations. They multiply the number of times a certain command us run. If you don't pay close attention to this, you will land yourself in trouble. Let's see an example of a nested until command inside a while loop.

```
cat #!/bin/bash

# I am nesting an until within a while loop

vart=3

until [ $vart -eq 0 ]

do

echo "This is the outer loop: $vart"

varx=1

while [ $varx -lt 5 ]

do

vary=`echo "scale=4; $vart / $varx" | bc`

echo " This is the Inner loop: $vart / $varx = $vary"

varx=$[ $varx + 1 ]

done
```

vart=$[$vart - 1]

done

$bash -f main.sh

This is the outer loop: 3

 Inner loop: 3 / 1 = 3.0000

 Inner loop: 3 / 2 = 1.5000

 Inner loop: 3 / 3 = 1.0000

 Inner loop: 3 / 4 = .7500

This is the outer loop: 2

 Inner loop: 2 / 1 = 2.0000

 Inner loop: 2 / 2 = 1.0000

 Inner loop: 2 / 3 = .6666

 Inner loop: 2 / 4 = .5000

This is the outer loop: 1

 Inner loop: 1 / 1 = 1.0000

 Inner loop: 1 / 2 = .5000

 Inner loop: 1 / 3 = .3333

 Inner loop: 1 / 4 = .2500

Nesting for Loop Inside for Loop

This is an example of nesting a for loop inside of another for loop.

```
cat
#!/bin/bash
# nesting the for loops
for (( x = 1; x <= 7; x++ ))
do
echo "Starting loop $x:"
for (( y = 1; y <= 7; y++ ))
do
echo " This is Inside the for loop: $y"
done
done
$bash -f main.sh
```

Starting loop 1:

    This is Inside the for loop: 1

    This is Inside the for loop: 2

    This is Inside the for loop: 3

    This is Inside the for loop: 4

    This is Inside the for loop: 5

    This is Inside the for loop: 6

    This is Inside the for loop: 7

Starting loop 2:

    This is Inside the for loop: 1

    This is Inside the for loop: 2

    This is Inside the for loop: 3

    This is Inside the for loop: 4

    This is Inside the for loop: 5

    This is Inside the for loop: 6

    This is Inside the for loop: 7

Starting loop 3:

    This is Inside the for loop: 1

    This is Inside the for loop: 2

    This is Inside the for loop: 3

    This is Inside the for loop: 4

    This is Inside the for loop: 5

    This is Inside the for loop: 6

    This is Inside the for loop: 7

Starting loop 4:

    This is Inside the for loop: 1

    This is Inside the for loop: 2

    This is Inside the for loop: 3

This is Inside the for loop: 4

This is Inside the for loop: 5

This is Inside the for loop: 6

This is Inside the for loop: 7

Starting loop 5:

This is Inside the for loop: 1

This is Inside the for loop: 2

This is Inside the for loop: 3

This is Inside the for loop: 4

This is Inside the for loop: 5

This is Inside the for loop: 6

This is Inside the for loop: 7

Starting loop 6:

This is Inside the for loop: 1

This is Inside the for loop: 2

This is Inside the for loop: 3

This is Inside the for loop: 4

This is Inside the for loop: 5

This is Inside the for loop: 6

This is Inside the for loop: 7

Starting loop 7:

> This is Inside the for loop: 1
>
> This is Inside the for loop: 2
>
> This is Inside the for loop: 3
>
> This is Inside the for loop: 4
>
> This is Inside the for loop: 5
>
> This is Inside the for loop: 6
>
> This is Inside the for loop: 7

More On Nested Loops

```
cat
#!/bin/bash
# This is to place a for loop inside a while loop
var4=10
while [ $var4 -ge 0 ]
do
echo "You seeing the value in the Outer loop: $var4"
for (( var5 = 1; $var5 < 3; var5++ ))
do
var6=$[ $var4 * $var5 ]
```

```
        echo "You seeing the value in the Inner loop: $var4 * $var5
= $var6"

    done

    var4=$[ $var4 - 1 ]

done

$bash -f main.sh
```

You seeing the value in the Outer loop: 10

You seeing the value in the Inner loop: 10 * 1 = 10

You seeing the value in the Inner loop: 10 * 2 = 20

You seeing the value in the Outer loop: 9

You seeing the value in the Inner loop: 9 * 1 = 9

You seeing the value in the Inner loop: 9 * 2 = 18

You seeing the value in the Outer loop: 8

You seeing the value in the Inner loop: 8 * 1 = 8

You seeing the value in the Inner loop: 8 * 2 = 16

You seeing the value in the Outer loop: 7

You seeing the value in the Inner loop: 7 * 1 = 7

You seeing the value in the Inner loop: 7 * 2 = 14

You seeing the value in the Outer loop: 6

You seeing the value in the Inner loop: 6 * 1 = 6

You seeing the value in the Inner loop: 6 * 2 = 12

You seeing the value in the Outer loop: 5

You seeing the value in the Inner loop: 5 * 1 = 5

You seeing the value in the Inner loop: 5 * 2 = 10

You seeing the value in the Outer loop: 4

You seeing the value in the Inner loop: 4 * 1 = 4

You seeing the value in the Inner loop: 4 * 2 = 8

You seeing the value in the Outer loop: 3

You seeing the value in the Inner loop: 3 * 1 = 3

You seeing the value in the Inner loop: 3 * 2 = 6

You seeing the value in the Outer loop: 2

You seeing the value in the Inner loop: 2 * 1 = 2

You seeing the value in the Inner loop: 2 * 2 = 4

You seeing the value in the Outer loop: 1

You seeing the value in the Inner loop: 1 * 1 = 1

You seeing the value in the Inner loop: 1 * 2 = 2

You seeing the value in the Outer loop: 0

You seeing the value in the Inner loop: 0 * 1 = 0

You seeing the value in the Inner loop: 0 * 2 = 0

The break Command

The break command is considered as the simplest way to exit a loop that is in progress. You can use it to exit all kinds of loops. When you are operating Linux, there comes a time when it is crucial to use the break command. The following section shows each method for the break command. Let's see how to do that.

When the shell receives the break command, and it executes it, it is breaking the loop. See how to use the break command.

```
cat #!/bin/bash

# This script is aimed at breaking out of loops

for vart in 1 2 3 4 5 6 7 8 9 10 11 12 13 14 15 16 17 18 19 20 21 22 23 24 25

do

if [ $vart -eq 5 ]

then

break

fi

echo "The ongoing iteration number is the following: $vart"

done

echo "The for loop reaches its end."

$bash -f main.sh

The ongoing iteration number is the following: 1

The ongoing iteration number is the following: 2

The ongoing iteration number is the following: 3
```

The ongoing iteration number is the following: 4

The for loop reaches its end.

Let's extend the scope of the break command. I will now break it at 18 numbers.

```
cat #!/bin/bash
# This script is aimed at breaking out of loops
for vart in 1 2 3 4 5 6 7 8 9 10 11 12 13 14 15 16 17 18 19 20 21 22 23 24 25
do
if [ $vart -eq 18 ]
then
break
fi
echo "The ongoing iteration number is the following: $vart"
done
echo "The for loop reaches its end."
$bash -f main.sh
The ongoing iteration number is the following: 1
The ongoing iteration number is the following: 2
The ongoing iteration number is the following: 3
The ongoing iteration number is the following: 4
```

The ongoing iteration number is the following: 5

The ongoing iteration number is the following: 6

The ongoing iteration number is the following: 7

The ongoing iteration number is the following: 8

The ongoing iteration number is the following: 9

The ongoing iteration number is the following: 10

The ongoing iteration number is the following: 11

The ongoing iteration number is the following: 12

The ongoing iteration number is the following: 13

The ongoing iteration number is the following: 14

The ongoing iteration number is the following: 15

The ongoing iteration number is the following: 16

The ongoing iteration number is the following: 17

The for loop reaches its end.

In the above two examples, you saw that the point where I installed the break command, the shell identified it, and executed it. Right at that point, the for loop ended, leaving the rest of the iteration to linger on. The break command works well for the while and until loops. Let's see how you can add them in the while and until loops. I will start with the while loop.

cat #!/bin/bash

```
# I will apply the break command to while loop

vart=1

while [ $vart -lt 25 ]

do

if [ $vart -eq 18 ]

then

break

fi

echo "The current Iteration number is as follows: $vart"

vart=$[ $vart + 1 ]

done
```

$bash -f main.sh

The current Iteration number is as follows: 1

The current Iteration number is as follows: 2

The current Iteration number is as follows: 3

The current Iteration number is as follows: 4

The current Iteration number is as follows: 5

The current Iteration number is as follows: 6

The current Iteration number is as follows: 7

The current Iteration number is as follows: 8

The current Iteration number is as follows: 9

The current Iteration number is as follows: 10

The current Iteration number is as follows: 11

The current Iteration number is as follows: 12

The current Iteration number is as follows: 13

The current Iteration number is as follows: 14

The current Iteration number is as follows: 15

The current Iteration number is as follows: 16

The current Iteration number is as follows: 17

Breaking out of Inner Loop

The break command has the power to terminate the inner loop. Let us see how to do that. There are two for loops in the next example. I will break out the inner for loop.

```
cat #!/bin/bash

# I will be breaking out of the inner loop

for (( x = 1; x < 4; x++ ))

do

echo "This is the Outer loop: $x"

for (( y = 1; y < 100; y++ ))

do

if [ $y -eq 15 ]

then
```

```
break

fi

echo " This is the Inner loop: $y"

done

done

$bash -f main.sh
```

This is the Outer loop: 1

 This is the Inner loop: 1

 This is the Inner loop: 2

 This is the Inner loop: 3

 This is the Inner loop: 4

 This is the Inner loop: 5

 This is the Inner loop: 6

 This is the Inner loop: 7

 This is the Inner loop: 8

 This is the Inner loop: 9

 This is the Inner loop: 10

 This is the Inner loop: 11

 This is the Inner loop: 12

 This is the Inner loop: 13

 This is the Inner loop: 14

This is the Outer loop: 2

This is the Inner loop: 1

This is the Inner loop: 2

This is the Inner loop: 3

This is the Inner loop: 4

This is the Inner loop: 5

This is the Inner loop: 6

This is the Inner loop: 7

This is the Inner loop: 8

This is the Inner loop: 9

This is the Inner loop: 10

This is the Inner loop: 11

This is the Inner loop: 12

This is the Inner loop: 13

This is the Inner loop: 14

This is the Outer loop: 3

This is the Inner loop: 1

This is the Inner loop: 2

This is the Inner loop: 3

This is the Inner loop: 4

This is the Inner loop: 5

This is the Inner loop: 6

This is the Inner loop: 7

This is the Inner loop: 8

This is the Inner loop: 9

This is the Inner loop: 10

This is the Inner loop: 11

This is the Inner loop: 12

This is the Inner loop: 13

This is the Inner loop: 14

You can see that each time the inner loop iterated, it broke out at the break command point.

Breaking Out of Outer Loop

There may come a time when it becomes necessary for you to stop the outer loop altogether instead of ceasing the iteration of the inner loop. The break command has a parameter value n that you can use to specify the level of the loop that you want to break out of. The n parameter, by default, indicates breaking out of the loop. If you set n to the value of two, it indicates that the break command will stop at the outer loop. Here is an example.

```
cat #!/bin/bash

# I am going to break out of the outer loop

for (( x = 1; x < 4; x++ ))
```

```
do

echo "This is the Outer loop: $x"

for (( y = 1; y < 100; y++ ))

do

if [ $y -gt 10 ]

then

break 2

fi

echo " This is the Inner loop: $y"

done

done

$bash -f main.sh

This is the Outer loop: 1

 This is the Inner loop: 1

 This is the Inner loop: 2

 This is the Inner loop: 3

 This is the Inner loop: 4

 This is the Inner loop: 5

 This is the Inner loop: 6

 This is the Inner loop: 7

 This is the Inner loop: 8
```

This is the Inner loop: 9

This is the Inner loop: 10

The break command broke the outer loop and kept it from iterating. You can notice the number '2' written beside the 'break' keyword. All the magic happened due to that number. If you remove it, you will let the outer loop complete its iteration. Let's see what happens if we remove that.

```
cat #!/bin/bash

# I am going to break out of the outer loop

for (( x = 1; x < 4; x++ ))

do

echo "This is the Outer loop: $x"

for (( y = 1; y < 100; y++ ))

do

if [ $y -gt 10 ]

then

break

fi

echo " This is the Inner loop: $y"

done

done
```

$bash -f main.sh

This is the Outer loop: 1

This is the Inner loop: 1

This is the Inner loop: 2

This is the Inner loop: 3

This is the Inner loop: 4

This is the Inner loop: 5

This is the Inner loop: 6

This is the Inner loop: 7

This is the Inner loop: 8

This is the Inner loop: 9

This is the Inner loop: 10

This is the Outer loop: 2

This is the Inner loop: 1

This is the Inner loop: 2

This is the Inner loop: 3

This is the Inner loop: 4

This is the Inner loop: 5

This is the Inner loop: 6

This is the Inner loop: 7

This is the Inner loop: 8

This is the Inner loop: 9

This is the Inner loop: 10

This is the Outer loop: 3

This is the Inner loop: 1

This is the Inner loop: 2

This is the Inner loop: 3

This is the Inner loop: 4

This is the Inner loop: 5

This is the Inner loop: 6

This is the Inner loop: 7

This is the Inner loop: 8

This is the Inner loop: 9

This is the Inner loop: 10

You can see how removing the small parameter has changed the entire structure of the script. Therefore, you must take care of the small nuances in shell scripting.

The Continue Command

The next on the line is the continue command, which is a way to stop the processing of a particular command within a loop but still avoiding to altogether terminating the loop. This will allow you to fix conditions inside of a loop where the shell is not executing commands. I will demonstrate the operations of this loop with the help of a practical example.

```
cat #!/bin/bash
# I will use the continue command in the loop
for (( vart = 1; vart < 20; vart++ ))
do
if [ $vart -gt 7 ] && [ $vart -lt 13 ]
then
continue
fi
echo "The ongoing Iteration number is as follows: $vart"
done
$bash -f main.sh
The ongoing Iteration number is as follows: 1
The ongoing Iteration number is as follows: 2
The ongoing Iteration number is as follows: 3
The ongoing Iteration number is as follows: 4
The ongoing Iteration number is as follows: 5
The ongoing Iteration number is as follows: 6
The ongoing Iteration number is as follows: 7
The ongoing Iteration number is as follows: 13
```

The ongoing Iteration number is as follows: 14

The ongoing Iteration number is as follows: 15

The ongoing Iteration number is as follows: 16

The ongoing Iteration number is as follows: 17

The ongoing Iteration number is as follows: 18

The ongoing Iteration number is as follows: 19

Please note that I installed the continue statement by directing it to stop at 7 and then continue at 13. You can see that the shell has excluded the range that I specified in the continue command. Just like the 'for' loop, you also can use the continue command in the while and the 'until' loop.

Processing Output

You can write a script that would process the output of a 'for' loop to a file.

```
cat #!/bin/bash

# Here you will learn to redirect output to a file

for (( x = 1; x < 10; x++ ))

do

echo "The output number is $x"

done > test1.txt

echo "The command had done its job."
```

The shell will create the file test1.txt and redirect the output to the file instead of displaying it on the shell screen.

The Case Command

```
cat test25 #!/bin/bash

# I am looking for value

if [ $USER = "rich" ]

then

echo "I say welcome to $USER"

echo "You must be enjoying your visit"

elif [ $USER = jessica ]

then

echo "I say welcome to $USER"

echo " I hope you are enjoying your visit"

elif [ $USER = testing ]

then

echo "This is a special testing account"

elif [ $USER = mona ]

then

echo "You must forget to log out once you're done"

else

echo "Sorry, I don't allow you."

fi
```

Chapter Nine

Advanced Shell Scripting

You saw how you can write scripts and manage data in Linux. The bash shell has some special parameters that are known as positional parameters to all the parameters that are entered in the command line. Sometimes your script is meant to be highly interactive. In that case, it is good to have the user input option in place. The shell offers you the read command for the purpose. The read command takes input from the keyboard or a file descriptor. After receiving the input, the read command reroutes the data toward a standard variable. Here is the read command in its simplest form.

Read Command

```
cat #!/bin/bash

# I am learning to test the read command

echo -n "You ought to enter your name here: "

read yourname
```
echo "Hello $yourname, I welcome you to my Linux system. You can do your work and then log out in the evening."

Functions

While you are writing shell scripts, you find yourself using the same code again and again. This is a waste of time and a cause of frustration as well. If the code is a small one, the level of frustration is likely to be low, but if the code is a large one, it is a problem. It will exhaust you and offend you. The bash shell offers user-defined functions that you can use to encapsulate the shell script inside of a function. Afterward, you can use the same as many times as you need it. This section of the chapter will walk you through Linux functions, which are an essential part of Linux administration. You will learn how to create them, how to use them in other script applications.

Functions are blocks of code that can be assigned a name and then reused in the code later on. All you need is to call out the name of the function in the shell script, and the function will activate. You can create a function by using the keyword function. A function has a defined unique name. You can add one or more commands to the code block of your function. When you make a function call, the bash shell will execute all commands of the function in the same order as they show up in the normal script.

cat #!/bin/bash

I am going to create and use a function in the following script

function func1 {

echo "This is a simple example of a shell function"

```
}
count=1
while [ $count -le 10 ]
do
func1
count=$[ $count + 1 ]
done
echo "Here the loop ends"
func1
echo "Here the scrip ends"
$bash -f main.sh
```

This is a simple example of a shell function

This is a simple example of a shell function

This is a simple example of a shell function

This is a simple example of a shell function

This is a simple example of a shell function

This is a simple example of a shell function

This is a simple example of a shell function

This is a simple example of a shell function

This is a simple example of a shell function

This is a simple example of a shell function

Here the loop ends

This is a simple example of a shell function

Here the scrip ends

The bash shell has included the function in the loop and iterated through it. If you try to use a function before you have defined it, you will receive an error message.

```
cat #!/bin/bash

# I am going to use a function that is located in the middle
of the script

count=1

echo "This line doesn't come under the umbrella of the
function definition"

function func1 {

echo "This is a simple example of a shell function"

}

while [ $count -le 15 ]

do

func1

count=$[ $count + 1 ]

done

echo "This just ends the loop"
```

func2

echo "This marks the end of the script"

function func2 {

echo "This is a simple example of a function"

}

$bash -f main.sh

This line doesn't come under the umbrella of the function definition

This is a simple example of a shell function

This is a simple example of a shell function

This is a simple example of a shell function

This is a simple example of a shell function

This is a simple example of a shell function

This is a simple example of a shell function

This is a simple example of a shell function

This is a simple example of a shell function

This is a simple example of a shell function

This is a simple example of a shell function

This is a simple example of a shell function

This is a simple example of a shell function

This is a simple example of a shell function

This is a simple example of a shell function

This is a simple example of a shell function

This just ends the loop

This marks the end of the script

main.sh: line 14: func2: command not found

You can see as the func2 was defined after the function call, I received an error message on the shell screen. Therefore, you need to be careful about it. Also, you need to be careful about the name of the functions. Otherwise, the latest function will override the previous function. The following example explains the gravity of choosing the right names of functions.

```
cat #!/bin/bash

# I am going to test the shell functions by using a duplicate function name

function func1 {

echo "This is my first definition of the first function."

}

func1

function func1 {

echo "This function carries the same name as of the previous function. It will override the first function."

}
```

```
func1

echo "This marks the end of the script."

$bash -f main.sh
```

This is my first definition of the first function.

This function carries the same name as of the previous function. It will override the first function.

This marks the end of the script.

Passing Parameters

The bash shell treats functions as mini-scripts. It means that you can pass a bunch of parameters to a function as a shell script. Functions will take the standard parameter environment variables for the representation of parameters that are passed to the function on your command line. For example, the name of the function can be defined in the $0 variable. You can add $1 and $2 as parameters to the same function.

```
cat #!/bin/bash

# I am passing a bunch of parameters to my function

function addthem {

if [ $# -eq 0 ] || [ $# -gt 9 ]

then

echo -1
```

```
elif [ $# -eq 1 ]
then
echo $[ $1 + $1 ]
else
echo $[ $1 + $2 ]
fi
}
echo -n "The shell is now adding 20 and 15: "
value=`addthem 20 15`
echo $value
echo -n "Now the shell is going to add just one number: "
value=`addthem 20`
echo $value
echo -n "Now the shell will add no numbers: "
value=`addthem`
echo $value
echo -n "Here the shell will add three numbers: "
value=`addthem 50 45 90`
echo $value
$bash -f main.sh
The shell is now adding 20 and 15: 35
```

Now the shell is going to add just one number: 40

Now the shell will add no numbers: -1

Here the shell will add three numbers: 95

The addthem function checks the parameters and adds them to compile the result. Since the function is using a special parameter environment variable for its values, it cannot access the script parameter values.

Function Variables

One major thing that can cause problems for programmers is defining the scope of a particular variable. The scope is at the position where a particular variable is visible. The variables that are defined inside functions have a different scope than regular variables, which is why they stay hidden from the rest of the shell script. Functions use two types of variables, such as global and local.

Global variables can be defined as the variables that stand valid at any position in a shell script. If you define one in the major section, you can retrieve it inside of another function. If you define it inside a function, you can retrieve it in the main section of your script. Any variables that you define in the script becomes a global variable.

cat

#!/bin/bash

```
function dbl {

value=$[ $value * 2 ]

}
```

read -p "You need to enter a value here: " value

dbl

echo "You new value is: $value"

Functions allow you to pass on arrays to the script. You need to disassemble an array into individual values and then use the same values as function parameters. Inside the function, you can always reassemble all the parameters inside a new array variable. Here is an example of the same.

```
cat

#!/bin/bash

# array variable to function test

function arrayit {

local newarray

newarray=(`echo "$@"`)

echo "The value of the new array is as follows: ${newarray[*]}"

}

myarray=(1 2 3 4 5 6 7 8 9 10 11 12 13 14 15)

echo "The value of the original array is ${myarray[*]}"
```

arrayit ${myarray[*]}

$bash -f main.sh

The value of the original array is 1 2 3 4 5 6 7 8 9 10 11 12 13 14 15

The value of the new array is as follows: 1 2 3 4 5 6 7 8 9 10 11 12 13 14 15

Function Recursion

One important feature that the location function variables offer is self-containment. A self-contained function doesn't use any of the resources outside of the shell function. The feature tends to enable the function that will, later on, be called recursively. Calling a function recursively means that when the function itself to get an answer. The classic example of a recursive algorithm is when you calculate the factorials. A factorial is the value of all the preceding numbers that are multiplied with the same number. See the following example:

5!=1*2*3*4*5-120

Chapter Ten

Coloring the Scripts

The most common method to add interactivity to the shell script is by adding colors to it. If you offer your customers a choice of different options, you will be able to be guided through what the script can and what it can't do.

Creating Menu

You can create your menu layout in Linux. The first step is to determine what elements you need to add to it. Then you should layout the way you want them to be displayed on the screen. Before you can create the menu, it is the best idea to clear the display of the monitor. This will enable you to display the menu in a much cleaner environment without distracting the text. You can use the echo command to display the printable text characters. When you are creating your menu items, it always is a good idea to use non-printable things such as tab as well as newline characters. Let's see the script to create a menu.

```
cat #!/bin/bash
# This is the way to a simple script menu
function dkspace {
clear
```

```
df -k

}

function whoon {

clear

who

}

function memusg {

clear

cat /proc/meminfo

}

function menu1 {

clear

echo

echo -e "\t\t\tThis is the System's Admin Menu\n"

echo -e "\t1. This area will display the disk space."

echo -e "\t2. This area will display logged on users"

echo -e "\t3. This area will display memory usage"

echo -e "\t0. This will Exit the program\n\n"

echo -en "\t\tYou are required to Enter an option: "

read -n 1 option

}
```

```
while [ 1 ]
do
menu1
case $option in
0)
break ;;
1)
dkspace ;;
2)
whoon ;;
3)
memusg ;;
*)
clear
echo "Sorry, you have made the wrong selection";;
esac
echo -en "\n\n\t\t\tPress a key from the keyboard to continue"
read -n 1 line
done
clear
$
```

The Select Command

You might have noticed that around half the problem is creating the layout while the other half is about retrieving the answer. The bash shell tends to provide a helpful utility. The select command will offer you to create a menu from a single command line, then retrieve the answer and process it. I will use the list parameter in the script.

```
cat #!/bin/bash

# I will be using the select command in the menu

function dkspace {

clear

df -k

}

function whoon {

clear

who

}

function memusg {

clear

cat /proc/meminfo

}

PS3="You are required to Enter an option here: "
```

```
select option in "This is the Display for the disk space" "This is the
Display for the logged on users"

        "This is the Display for the memory usage" "You can Exit
        the program now"

        do

        case $option in

        "You can Exit the program now")

        break ;;

        "This is the Display for the disk space")

        diskspace ;;

        "This is the Display for the logged on users")

        whoseon ;;

        "This is the Display for the memory usage")

        memusage ;;

        *)

        clear

        echo "Sorry, you have made the wrong selection";;

        esac

        done

        clear

        $
```

Using Color in Scripts

You can add ANSI escape control code in the shell scripts to further control the format of the script output. This is useful when you are using menus. You can change the color at will.

```
cat #!/bin/bash

# This is to add colors to the menu using ANSI colors

function dkspace {

clear

df -k

}

function whoon {

clear

who

}

function memusg {

clear

cat /proc/meminfo

}

function menu1 {

clear

echo
```

```
echo -e "\t\t\tThis is the System's Admin Menu\n"

echo -e "\t1. This will Display the disk space"

echo -e "\t2. This will Display the logged on users space"

echo -e "\t3. This will Display the memory usage"

echo -e "^[[1m\t0. You can Exit the program
here\n\n^[[0m^[[44;33m"

echo -en "\t\tPlease Enter an option here: "

read -n 1 option

}

echo "^[[44;33m"

while [ 1 ]

do

menu1

case $option in

0)

break ;;

1)

dkspace ;;

2)

whoon ;;

3)
```

```
memusg ;;

*)

clear

echo -e "^[[5m\t\t\tSorry, you have made the wrong
selection^[[0m^[[44;33m";; esac

echo -en "\n\n\t\t\tYou should pres a key from the keyboard
in order to continue"

read -n 1 line

done

echo "^[[0m"

clear

$
```

Chapter Eleven

A Simple Linux Shell Script Program

Calculator

```
echo "What is the number on your brain?"

read num1

echo "what is the second number on your brain?"

read num2

echo "what mathematical operator do you want to use?"

echo "1. addion"

echo "2. subtraction"

echo "3. division"

echo "4. multiplication"

read ans

if

ans=$(( $num1+$num2 )); then

echo $ans

elif

ans=$(( $num1-$num2 )); then
```

echo $ans

elif

ans=$(($num1/$num2)); then

echo $ans

elif

ans=$(($num1*$num2)); then

echo $ans

else

$bash -f main.sh

What is the number on your brain?

what is the second number on your brain?

what mathematical operator do you want to use?

    1. addion

    2. subtraction

    3. division

    4. multiplication

Conclusion

Now that you have made it to the end of the book, I hope you have digested enough knowledge about Linux that you can appreciate the advantages of using Linux as your primary operating system. Linux is amazing because you do not have to spend a hefty sum of cash on purchasing license keys just as with Windows. If you are looking forward to buying the Windows license for personal use, it will not appear to be costly, but if you want to buy the key for a business, you will need it for a bunch of employees, which will scale up the cost. You will also have to pay for the attached applications such as MS Office, Sharepoint, Exchange that are native to the Windows operating system.

The worst part about using the Windows system is that you do not get the freedom to modify it. Similarly, you cannot modify or customize the applications as well. This means you have to follow the same beaten track that others have been treading for a while. With Linux, you can download the source code of the entire operating system without burning a hole in your pocket. Although a few Linux distributions do charge some money, it is inexpensive as compared to the Windows license key.

Linux is viewed as the most reliable operating system as compared to Windows. Linux is likely to rock with the latest top-notch designs and built-in high-profile security measures. The developers of Linux distributions are quite active, and they keep releasing off and on some major and minor updates. Linux systems have got the reputation of running on a wide range of hardware systems without a failure.

Although Linux demands a high-end computer system if you have to use it for programming, the scale of RAM and Storage is much lower than that of Windows. Hardware vendors are gradually realizing the importance and popularity of Linux operating systems; hence they have started manufacturing Linux compliant drivers and hardware.

The fact cannot be denied that Windows enjoy the support of a big number of commercial software. On the other hand, Linux can make use of open-source software that comes for free. You can get hands-on nice desktop themes that run faster than their Windows counterparts. Linux terminal tends to offer a finer environment than that of Windows.

Windows operating system is full of vulnerabilities of different kinds, such as hacking attacks and alike things. However, Linux is not as vulnerable to attacks as Windows is. It cannot be said that Linux has a foolproof security system that even a determined hacker cannot break; however, its system is more secure. The security of Linux comes from the way Linux works. Microsoft Windows is vulnerable to trojans, ransomware, viruses, and malware. Linux does not need any anti-malware or anti-virus software.

The best thing about a Linux operating system is that you can install it and use it as a file server, a desktop, a web server, a firewall, and much more. These are just so many facilities. A Windows operating system does not offer any such thing to users. A Linux is well-known as an open-source operating system which allows you to modify the sources of applications as per your custom requirements. This is what makes it amazing. You can install only the software you need. There is no forceful installation of software on your system, unlike Windows. Windows are designed in a way that will cause boredom one day because of its default desktop themes and a set color scheme that has limited change options. Linux allows you to choose from a wide range of desktop themes that are available for you.

Are you just fed up with the crashes and reboots on your Windows operating system? Everyone is, at some point in their journey with the Windows operating system. Windows is unpredictable in its tendency to show annoying messages that say that the machine needs a reboot. You have to wrap up all the work in a matter of seconds, close all the tabs and let the unwelcome intruding instructions to take over the controls on the system. It just feels as if you are losing control, and someone else has taken over the system for a while as you are shut out of the system.

The most annoying thing, if you agree with me, is the update feature. The update window would pop up from time to time on the screen, demand you restart the machine, and start applying a long list of updates. I cannot remember if any update session had ended before the completion of 30 minutes. Windows also confuse the user by mixing up an update of service packs, features, security updates, and a set of tools. It just keeps rebooting when it detects and downloads an update from the internet. When you are updating software or uninstalling it on Linux systems, it will not need a reboot in the first place. Most configuration changes you make can be done when the system is running.

As your operating systems evolve, your hardware requirements also evolve in the same manner. Windows operating systems demand fulfillment of minimum requirements for hardware, which means that you will have to upgrade your hardware to a high-end system. It is Linux that can help you utilize your old computers. This does not mean that all Linux administrations would be fine with a 256 MB RAM. However, if you do not have access to a high-end computer, you can install Linux on a low-end system and do some urgent work. If you compare a high-end Windows system and a high-end Linux system, the Linux distribution will have an edge. This is why most servers across the world prefer Linux over Windows.

If you are an aspiring programmer, you will be happy to know that Linux supports major programming languages like Python, Perl, C, C++, and Ruby. It also offers many applications which a programmer finds useful. The Linux terminal of which I have given you a detailed account is considered way superior for use over its Windows counterpart, the command line. Developers find it efficient, user-friendly, and fast. Many libraries are natively developed in Linux. Programmers agree that the package manager of Linux helps them in getting things done easily. Bash scripting, which I have discussed in a comprehensive, is the most attractive thing about Linux. Developers love it and consider it the reason for their ditching Windows. As if everything else was not enough to lure in computer users, Linux has native support for SSH, which means that you can manage different servers on Linux faster than that of other operating systems.

Windows, if it gets corrupted, needs to be fixed by an expert who would charge a heavy fee from you. However, you do not have to hire an expert if your Linux system runs into a stumbling block. All you need is to search the error on the web and look out for a solution. Within a few minutes, you will find it. If you cannot find it, the problem is likely to be a new one. Therefore post a thread on Linux forums, and you will receive a reply with a detailed solution, which would help you resolve the problem. This comes at without any additional cost. Lots of Linux users remain ready to respond to queries in the relevant thread. This has resulted in a giant pool of queries and solutions, making Linux community one of the liveliest communities in the tech world. The Linux community is bigger than the Windows community.

Moreover, a majority of Linux community members are real tech-brains who are always looking out to help people who face problems in Linux administration. The biggest problem with Windows is that it tends to scale down its performance over time. It gets sluggish day by day. Therefore Linux comes as the most viable solution to these rising problems.

You have learned what Linux is and what the Linux terminal is. I explained in detail different sets of commands that you can enter in the shell and make daily processes easy and fun. I have explained how you can pace up your daily work in Linux by memorizing some keyboard tricks. Linux is the simplest and lightest yet the speediest operating system for users. It is not as much graphical as Windows is, but this is what makes Linux different from the rest of the lot. It thrives on the command line, the Linux shell. It allows you to wrap up complex and tangled operations in the fastest possible manner. I have also explained the ins and outs of shell scripting, which is the most attractive thing for programmers. You learned how to write shell scripts and customize the Linux interface. You can use this knowledge to get better at operating Linux and writing scripts. The most interesting thing is that you also can write your programs once you get command over writing shell scripts. You may get frustrated a bit at the start as it is not appealing to work on the shell screen and using a keyboard instead of a mouse, but gradually you will be quite at home with all this.

Resources

https://www.thegeekstuff.com/2010/06/bash-if-statement-examples/

https://www.geeksforgeeks.org/conditional-statements-shell-script/

https://www.oreilly.com/library/view/running-linux-third/156592469X/ch01s02.html

https://unix.stackexchange.com/questions/208639/how-create-calculator-in-linux-script

https://www.oreilly.com/library/view/running-linux-third/156592469X/ch01s02.html

https://wiki.lib.sun.ac.za/images/c/ca/TLCL-13.07.pdf

http://inf.ocs.ku.ac.th/Download/Wiley.Linux.Command.Line.and.Shell.Scripting.Bible.May.2008.pdf

http://index-of.es/Varios-2/How%20Linux%20Works%20What%20Every%20Superuser%20Should%20Know.pdf

www.ingramcontent.com/pod-product-compliance
Lightning Source LLC
LaVergne TN
LVHW022316060326
832902LV00020B/3497